Mediterranean Cookbook: 120 Family-Friendly Soup, Salad, Main Dish, Breakfast and Dessert Recipes for Better Health and Natural Weight Loss

by **Vesela Tabakova**

CW01499385

Table Of Contents

Delicious Whole Food Recipes For Better Living

The Mediterranean way of life is relaxed and family-oriented. Living, cooking and eating are joyous, shared activities. In the Mediterranean countries eating means sharing food and conversation with someone. And cooking means preparing delicious meals for your family and friends, so you can all gather around the table and enjoy food together. A fundamental characteristic of Mediterranean cuisine is that food is cooked using easily available ingredients - local, everyday products that we can buy around the corner or grow in our own backyard.

All my Mediterranean recipes are easy and healthy because they include olive oil, fresh vegetables, protein-rich legumes, whole grains, and aromatic herbs and spices. The cooked meals are generally prepared slowly, all in one pot, starting by gently sautéing meat and aromatic vegetables like onion and garlic, carrots and celery. Vegetable broth or wine is then added, followed by herbs, spices, grains, beans, pasta and vegetables. The principle is to add the ingredients, which need the shortest cooking time, last.

The health benefits of the Mediterranean diet are well known, proven with research and hard to ignore. A recent, large study of 7,500 people in Spain found that following a Mediterranean diet can cut the risk of heart disease-related deaths by about 30 percent compared to a typical Western diet. Changing your food habits and eating the way people in the Mediterranean do will greatly improve your health and you would be less likely to develop high blood pressure, high cholesterol, or become obese.

If you want to change your eating habits and at the same time reduce grocery costs, try some of my Mediterranean Recipes.

Just remember these rules to be certain that you are really following a Mediterranean diet:

Use olive oil when cooking. Use little or no butter at all;

Serve vegetables with every meal and eat fresh fruit every day. Fresh and dried fruit, nuts and seeds are excellent as snacks and desserts;

Include at least two legume meals per week;

Include at least two servings of fish per week;

Eat smaller portions of lean beef, lamb, pork and chicken. Deli, luncheon and cured meats are almost never eaten in the Mediterranean;

Eat yogurt and cheese in moderation;

Include wholegrain breads and cereals with meals;

Consume wine in moderation, only with meals.

Mediterranean Salad Recipes

Warm Italian Beef and Spinach Salad

Serves 4

Ingredients:

8 oz deli Italian roast beef, cut into 1/4 inch strips

1 red onion, sliced and separated into rings

2 tomatoes, sliced

1 red pepper, sliced

6 cups baby spinach leaves or torn fresh spinach

2 tbsp olive oil

1/2 cup grated Parmesan cheese, to serve

for the dressing:

1/2 cup sour cream

1 tbsp mustard

2 garlic cloves, pressed

Directions:

Stir together all dressing ingredients in a deep bowl and set aside.

Warm olive oil in a large skillet and sauté the beef and onions. Cook for 3-4 minutes, stirring occasionally, over medium heat, until the beef is heated through.

Toss together beef, spinach, tomatoes, red pepper and dressing in a large salad bowl. Serve sprinkled with Parmesan cheese.

Mediterranean Steak Salad

Serves 4

Ingredients:

1 lb boneless beef sirloin steak, 1 inch thick

4 cups, romaine or rocket leaves

1 red onion, sliced and separated into rings

1 cup cherry tomatoes, halved

1/2 cup green olives, pitted

1/2 feta cheese, crumbled

1 tsp salt

1/2 tsp black pepper

for the dressing:

3 garlic cloves, pressed

5 tbsp olive oil

5 tbsp lemon juice

1 tsp lemon zest

1/2 tsp dried thyme

Directions:

Prepare the dressing by combining all ingredients in a bowl.

Heat a heavy skillet. Season the steak with salt and ground black pepper. Cook it for 3-4 minutes on medium heat, then turn it and cook for 3-4 minutes more. Transfer the steak to a cutting board and leave it to cool. Slice it thinly.

Divide the romaine lettuce among 4 plates. Top with sliced meat, red onion, tomatoes, olives and feta cheese. Drizzle with dressing.

Mediterranean Beef Salad

Serves 4

Ingredients:

8 oz roast beef, thinly sliced

6 cups assorted greens, torn

1 cucumber, peeled and cut

6-7 white button mushrooms, thinly sliced

4 tbsp fresh basil leaves, torn

2 tbsp balsamic vinegar

4 tbsp olive oil

1 tsp salt

Directions:

Prepare the dressing by mixing vinegar, olive oil, garlic, salt and basil leaves in a bowl.

Divide greens among four plates. Arrange beef with cucumbers and mushrooms on top. Drizzle with the dressing and toss to combine.

Chicken, Broccoli and Cashew Salad

Serves 6

Ingredients:

1 lb fresh broccoli, cut into florets

9 oz grilled, boneless chicken breast, diced

3.5 oz cashews, baked

3.5 oz sunflower seeds, salted and baked

2 tbsp Parmesan cheese, grated

1/3 cup fresh parsley leaves, finely chopped

2 tbsp olive oil

2 tbsp lemon juice

Directions:

Wash the broccoli and steam it for 5 min until just tender, then tip into a large bowl. Set aside to cool and mix with the chicken. Add the cashews, the sunflower seeds and the finely cut parsley.

In a smaller cup, mix the olive oil and lemon juice. Pour over the salad and serve sprinkled with Parmesan cheese.

Italian Chicken Salad

Serves 4

Ingredients:

2 roasted or poached chicken breasts, shredded

2 yellow or orange bell peppers, thinly sliced

1 small red onion, thinly sliced

1 medium celery rib, chopped

1/4 cup slivered almonds, toasted

1 tbsp drained capers

juice of one lemon

1 tsp fresh thyme, minced

1/2 cup of Parmesan cheese

1/4 cup olive oil

1 tbsp Dijon mustard

1 tsp sugar

salt and pepper, to taste

Directions:

Combine vegetables and chicken in a salad bowl. Prepare the dressing by mixing the olive oil, lemon juice, mustard, sugar, salt and pepper.

Pour over the salad, toss well to combine, and serve.

Chicken and Avocado Salad

Serves 4

Ingredients:

2 cups grilled skinless, boneless chicken breast, diced

2 avocados, peeled, pitted and diced

1 red onion, finely chopped

1/2 cup green olives, pitted

10 cherry tomatoes, halved

2 tbsp lemon juice

3 tbsp olive oil

1 tsp oregano

salt and black pepper, to taste

Directions:

In a medium bowl, combine the avocados, chicken, onion and cherry tomatoes. Season with oregano, salt and pepper to taste.

Add the olives, lemon juice and olive oil and toss lightly to coat.

Chicken and Egg Salad

Serves 6

Ingredients:

2 cups cooked chicken, chopped

2 hard boiled eggs, diced

2-3 pickled gherkins, chopped

1 large apple, diced

1/2 cup walnuts, baked

1/2 cup light mayonnaise

1 tbsp lemon juice

salt and pepper, to taste

Directions:

Bake the walnuts in a single layer in a preheated to 450 F oven for 3 minutes, or until toasted and fragrant, stirring halfway through.

Stir together chicken, apple, eggs and gherkins. Combine mayonnaise, lemon juice, salt and pepper to taste, and add to the chicken mixture. Sprinkle with walnuts and serve.

Mediterranean Chicken Pasta Salad

Serves 6-8

Ingredients:

3 cups farfalle pasta, cooked

1 small roasted chicken, skin and bones removed, shredded

1 cup cherry tomatoes

1 cucumber, halved, sliced

1 red bell pepper, sliced

1 small red onion, sliced

1/2 cup fresh basil leaves, finely chopped

1/2 cup parsley leaves, finely chopped

1/2 cup black olives, pitted

1/3 cup pine nuts, toasted

for the dressing

1/3 cup red wine vinegar

1/4 cup olive oil

1 garlic clove, pressed

Directions:

Place pasta, chicken, tomato, cucumber, bell pepper, onion, basil, parsley, olives and pine nuts in a large bowl.

Make the dressing by combining vinegar, oil, garlic and salt. Pour the dressing over salad and toss to combine.

Greek Chicken Salad

Serves 4

Ingredients:

4 small chicken breast halves

1/3 cup white wine

1 tbsp lemon juice

1-2 tsp chopped fresh rosemary

3 garlic cloves, pressed

1/4 cup olive oil

2 tomatoes, cut into thin wedges

1 small red onion, cut into thin wedges

1/4 cup black olives

3.5 oz feta, crumbled

1/4 cup parsley leaves, chopped

4 pita bread, warmed, to serve

Directions:

Prepare a dressing from the white wine, lemon juice, garlic, rosemary and olive oil. Place chicken fillets in a bowl with half the dressing. Stir well and marinate for at least 15 minutes.

Heat a char-grill pan or non-stick frying pan over medium-high heat. Cook the chicken for 5 minutes each side until golden and cooked through. Set aside, covered with foil.

Toss the tomatoes, onion, olives, feta and parsley in the remaining dressing. Slice the chicken thickly and add to the salad, then toss gently to combine. Serve with pita bread.

Fresh Greens Salad

Serves 6-8

Ingredients:

1 head red leaf lettuce, rinsed, dried and chopped

1 head green leaf lettuce, rinsed, dried, and chopped

1 head endive, rinsed, dried and chopped

1 cup frisee lettuce leaves, rinsed, dried, and chopped

3 leaves fresh basil, chopped

3 sprigs fresh mint, chopped

4 tbsp olive oil

2 tbsp lemon juice

1 tbsp honey

salt, to taste

Directions:

Place the red and green leaf lettuce, frisee lettuce, endive, basil and mint into a large salad bowl, and toss lightly to combine.

Prepare the dressing from the lemon juice, the olive oil and the honey and pour over the salad. Season with salt to taste.

Caprese Salad

Serves 6

Ingredients:

4 tomatoes, sliced

5.5 oz mozzarella cheese, sliced

10 fresh basil leaves

3 tbsp olive oil

2 tbsp balsamic vinegar

salt, to taste

Directions:

Slice the tomatoes and mozzarella, then layer the tomato slices, whole fresh basil leaves and mozzarella slices on a plate.

Drizzle olive oil and balsamic vinegar over the salad and serve.

Beet and Bean Sprout Salad

Serves 4

Ingredients:

7 beet greens, finely sliced

2 medium tomatoes, sliced

1 cup bean sprouts, washed

1 tbsp grated lemon rind

2 garlic cloves, pressed

1/2 cup lemon juice

1/2 cup olive oil

1 tsp salt

Directions:

In a large bowl, toss together beet greens, bean sprouts, tomatoes, and dressing.

Mix oil and lemon juice with lemon rind, salt and garlic and pour over the salad. Refrigerate for 2 hours to allow flavor to develop before serving. Serve chilled.

Baby Spinach Salad

Serves 4

Ingredients:

1 bag baby spinach, washed and dried

9 oz feta cheese, coarsely crumbled

1 red bell pepper, cut in slices

1 cup cherry tomatoes, cut in halves

1 red onion, finely chopped

1 cup black olives, pitted

1 tsp dried oregano

1 large garlic clove

3 tbsp red wine vinegar

4 tbsp olive oil

salt and freshly ground black pepper, to taste

Directions:

Prepare the dressing by blending the garlic and the oregano with the olive oil and the vinegar in a food processor.

Place the spinach leaves in a large salad bowl and toss with the dressing. Add the rest of the ingredients and give everything a toss again. Season to taste with black pepper and salt.

Tabbouleh

Serves 4-5

Ingredients:

1 cup raw bulgur

2 cups boiling water

3 cups finely cut parsley

2 tomatoes, chopped

2 garlic cloves, minced

6-7 spring onions, chopped

1 tbsp fresh mint leaves, chopped

3 tbsp olive oil

juice of two lemons

salt and black pepper, to taste

Directions:

Bring water and salt to a boil, then pour over bulgur. Cover and set aside for 15 minutes to steam. Drain excess water from bulgur and fluff with a fork. Leave to chill.

In a large bowl, mix together the parsley, tomatoes, olive oil, garlic, spring onions and mint. Stir in the chilled bulgur and season to taste with salt, pepper and lemon juice.

Fatoush

Serves 6

Ingredients:

2 cups lettuce, washed, dried, and chopped

3 tomatoes, chopped

1 cucumber, peeled and chopped

1 green pepper, seeded and chopped

1/2 cup radishes, sliced

1 small red onion, finely chopped

1/2 cup finely cut parsley

2 tbsp finely chopped fresh mint

3 tbsp olive oil

4 tbsp lemon juice

salt and black pepper, to taste

2 whole wheat pita breads

Directions:

Toast the pita breads in a skillet until they are browned and crisp. Set aside.

Place the lettuce, tomatoes, cucumbers, green pepper, radishes, onion, parsley and mint in a salad bowl. Break up the toasted pita into bite-size pieces and add to the salad.

Make the dressing by whisking together the olive oil with the lemon juice, a pinch of salt and some black pepper. Toss everything together until it is well coated with dressing and serve.

Greek Salad with Avocado

Serves 6

Ingredients:

2 cucumbers, diced

2 tomatoes, sliced

1 green lettuce, cut

2 red bell peppers, cut

1/2 cup olives, pitted

6 oz feta cheese, cut

1 red onion, sliced

1 avocado, peeled and diced

2 tbsp olive oil

2 tbsp lemon juice

salt and ground black pepper, to taste

Directions:

Dice the cucumbers and slice the tomatoes. Tear the lettuce or cut it in thin strips. De-seed and cut the peppers in strips. Dice the avocado.

Mix all vegetables in a salad bowl. Add the olives and the feta cheese cut in cubes. In a small cup mix the olive oil and the lemon juice with salt and pepper. Pour over the salad and stir again.

Tuna Salad

Serves 4

Ingredients:

1 head green lettuce, washed and drained

1 cucumber, cut

1 can tuna, drained and broken into small chunks

1/2 cup sweet corn, from a can

6-7 radishes, sliced

6-7 spring onions, finely cut

the juice of half a lemon or 2 tbsp of white wine vinegar

3 tbsp sunflower or olive oil

salt, to taste

Directions:

Cut the lettuce into thin strips. Slice the cucumber and the radishes as thinly as possible and chop the spring onions.

Mix all the vegetables in a large bowl, add the tuna and the sweet corn and season with lemon juice, oil and salt to taste.

Greek Chickpea Salad

Serves 4

Ingredients:

1 cup canned chickpeas, drained and rinsed

1 spring onion, thinly sliced

1 small cucumber, deseeded and diced

2 green bell peppers, diced

2 tomatoes, diced

2 tbsp chopped fresh parsley

1 tsp capers, drained and rinsed

juice of 1/2 lemon

2 tsp olive oil

1 tsp balsamic vinegar

salt and pepper, to taste

1/2 tsp oregano

Directions:

In a medium bowl, toss together the chickpeas, spring onion, cucumber, bell pepper, tomato, parsley, capers, and lemon juice.

In a smaller bowl, stir together the remaining ingredients and pour over the chickpea salad. Toss well to coat and allow to marinate, stirring occasionally, for at least 1 hour before serving.

Red Cabbage Salad

Serves 6

Ingredients:

1 small head red cabbage, cored and chopped

1/2 cup finely cut fresh dill

3 tbsp sunflower oil

3 tbsp red wine vinegar

1 tsp sugar

2 tsp salt

black pepper, to taste

Directions:

In a bowl, mix the oil, red wine vinegar sugar and black pepper. Place the cabbage in a large glass bowl. Sprinkle the salt on top and crunch it with your hands to soften.

Pour dressing over the cabbage, and toss to coat. Sprinkle the salad with the dill, cover it with foil, and leave it in the refrigerator for half an hour before serving.

Shepherds' Salad

Serves 6

Ingredients:

5-6 tomatoes, diced

2 cucumbers, sliced

5-6 white button mushrooms, sliced

2 red bell peppers, sliced

7 oz ham, diced

1 small onion, chopped

4 eggs, boiled and sliced

7 oz feta cheese, grated

1/2 cup finely cut parsley

4 tbsp olive oil

1 tbsp red wine vinegar

1 tsp salt

20-30 black olives, to serve

Directions:

Cut the tomatoes in small cubes. Cut the cucumber and the peppers in rings, chop the onion, thinly slice the mushrooms. Cut the ham. Combine the prepared ingredients in a salad bowl; drizzle with the olive oil and vinegar. Add salt, then mix well.

Divide the salad in 6 plates and sprinkle with the grated feta cheese and finely chopped parsley. Boil the eggs for 10 min, then cut them in discs. Garnish the salads with egg slices and olives. Serve chilled.

Okra Salad

Serves 4

Ingredients:

1.2 lb young okras

2 tomatoes, sliced

1 lemon

1/2 cup finely cut parsley

3 tbsp sunflower oil

1/2 tsp black pepper

salt, to taste

Directions:

Trim okras, wash and cook in salted water. Drain and cool when tender.

In a small bowl, mix well the lemon juice and sunflower oil, salt and pepper. Pour over okras arranged in a bowl and sprinkle with chopped parsley. Serve garnished with tomato slices.

Cucumber Salad

Serves 4

Ingredients:

2 medium cucumbers, peeled and sliced

1/2 cup finely cut dill

2 garlic cloves, pressed

3 tbsp white vinegar

5 tbsp olive oil

salt, to taste

Directions:

Cut the cucumbers in rings and put them in a salad bowl. Add the finely cut dill, the pressed garlic and season with salt, vinegar and oil.

Toss to combine and serve.

Simple Beetroot Salad

Serves 4

Ingredients:

2-3 small beets, peeled

3 spring onions, cut

3 cloves garlic, pressed

2 tbsp red vinegar

2-3 tbsp sunflower oil

salt, to taste

Directions:

Place the beats in a steam basket set over a pot of boiling water. Steam for about 12-15 minutes, or until tender. Leave to cool.

Grate the beets and put them in a salad bowl. Add the garlic cloves, the finely cut spring onions and mix well. Season with salt, vinegar and sunflower oil.

Mediterranean Soup Recipes

Italian Wedding Soup

Serves 5-6

Ingredients:

1 lb lean ground beef

1/3 cup breadcrumbs

1 egg, lightly beaten

1 onion, grated

2 carrots, chopped

1 small head escarole, trimmed and cut into 1/2 inch strips

1 cup baby spinach leaves

1/2 cup small pasta

2 tbsp Parmesan cheese, grated

2 tbsp parsley, finely cut

1 tsp salt

1 tsp ground black pepper

3 tbsp olive oil

3 cups chicken broth

3 cups water

1 tsp oregano

Directions:

Combine ground beef, egg, onion, breadcrumbs, cheese, parsley, 1/2 teaspoon of the salt and 1/2 teaspoon of the black pepper. Mix well with hands.

Using a tablespoon, make walnut sized meatballs. Heat olive oil in a large skillet and brown meatballs in batches. Place aside on a plate.

In a large soup pot, boil broth and water, together with carrots, oregano and the remaining salt and pepper. Gently add the meatballs. Reduce heat and simmer for 30 minutes. Add pasta, spinach and escarole and simmer for 10 more minutes.

Lentil and Beef Soup

Serves 5-6

Ingredients:

1 lb ground beef

1 cup brown lentils

2 carrots, chopped

2 onions, chopped

1 potato, cut into 1/2 inch cubes

4 garlic cloves, chopped

2 tomatoes, grated or pureed

5 cups water

1 tsp savory

1 tsp oregano

1 tsp paprika

2 tbsp olive oil

1 tsp salt

black pepper, to taste

Directions:

Heat olive oil in a large soup pot. Brown beef, breaking it up with a spoon. Add paprika and garlic and stir. Add lentils, the remaining vegetables, water and spice.

Bring to the boil. Reduce heat to low and simmer, covered, for about an hour, or until lentils are tender. Stir occasionally.

Beef and Vegetable Soup

Serves 8

Ingredients:

2 lbs stewing beef

3 tbsp olive oil

1 large onion, chopped

4-5 white button mushrooms, chopped

2 carrots, chopped

1 celery rib, chopped

1/2 cup dry white wine

6 cups water

2 tbsp tomato paste

1/2 cup parsley, chopped

salt and black pepper, to taste

Directions:

Season the beef pieces with salt and pepper. In a large soup pot, heat olive oil and seal the beef in batches, then set it aside in a plate, covered. Sauté the onions, mushrooms, carrots and celery over medium-high heat. Add the wine, stir, and return the meat to the pot. Add water and bring to the boil. Reduce heat and simmer, covered, for about an hour, stirring occasionally.

Dissolve the tomato paste in a few tablespoons of the soup and add it to the pot. Stir in the chopped parsley and season with salt and pepper to taste.

Beef and Vegetable Minestrone

Serves 6-7

Ingredients:

2 slices bacon, chopped

1 cup ground beef

2 carrots, chopped

2 cloves garlic, finely chopped

1 large onion, chopped

1 celery rib, chopped

1 can tomatoes, chopped

6 cups beef broth

1 can chickpeas, drained

1/2 cup small pasta

1 bay leaf

1 tsp dried basil

1 tsp dried rosemary

1/4 tsp crushed chillies

Directions:

In a large saucepan, cook bacon and ground beef until well done, breaking up the beef as it cooks. Drain off the fat and add carrots, garlic, onion and celery. Cook for about five minutes or until the onions are translucent. Season with basil, bay leaf, rosemary and crushed chillies. Stir in the tomatoes and beef broth.

Bring to a boil then reduce heat and simmer for about 20 minutes. Add in the chickpeas and pasta. Cook, uncovered, for about 10 minutes, or until the pasta is ready.

Italian Meatball Soup

Serves 6-7

Ingredients:

1 lb lean ground beef

1 small onion, grated

1 onion, chopped

2 garlic cloves, pressed

1 zucchini, peeled and diced

1/2 cup green beans, trimmed, cut into thirds

1/2 cup breadcrumbs

3-4 basil leaves, finely chopped

1/3 cup Parmesan cheese, grated

1 egg, lightly beaten

2 cups tomato sauce with basil

3 cups water

1/2 cup small pasta

2 tbsp olive oil

salt and black pepper, to taste

Directions:

Combine ground beef, grated onion, garlic, breadcrumbs, basil, Parmesan and egg in a large bowl. Season with salt and pepper. Mix well with hands and roll tablespoonfuls of the mixture into balls. Place on a large plate.

Heat olive oil in a large, deep saucepan and sauté onion and garlic until transparent. Add tomato sauce, water and bring to the boil over high heat. Add in meatballs.

Reduce heat to medium-low and simmer, uncovered, for 10 minutes. Add pasta and cook for 5 more minutes. Add the zucchini and beans. Cook until the pasta and vegetables are tender. Serve sprinkled with Parmesan cheese.

Mediterranean Chicken Soup

Serves 6-8

Ingredients:

about 1.5 lb chicken breasts

3-4 carrots, chopped

1 celery rib, chopped

1 red onion, chopped

1/3 cup rice

8 cups water

10 black olives, pitted and halved

fresh parsley or cilantro, to serve

1/2 tsp salt

ground black pepper, to taste

lemon juice, to serve

Directions:

Place chicken breasts in a soup pot. Add onion, carrots, celery, salt, pepper and water. Stir well and bring to a boil. Add rice, olives, stir and reduce heat. Simmer for 30-40 minutes.

Remove chicken from pot and let it cool slightly. Shred it and return it to pot. Serve soup with lemon juice and sprinkled with fresh parsley or cilantro.

Turkish Chicken Soup

Serves 6

Ingredients:

about 1.5 lb chicken breasts

4 tbsp butter

3 tbsp flour

3 cups of milk

4 cups water

1 tsp paprika

salt and ground black pepper, to taste

Directions:

Boil the chicken breasts in 4 cups of water for 30 minutes, or until cooked through. Remove chicken from the soup pot and leave it in a plate to cool. When cool enough shred and leave it aside.

Melt one tablespoon of butter with three tablespoons of flour in a small pan. Mix flour and butter well and cook until the mixture begins to brown, then remove from heat. Bring the chicken broth to a boil. Strain the flour and butter mixture in a strainer and stir into the soup. Add the shredded chicken and 3-4 cups of milk (depending on how thick you want the soup). Bring to the boil again and simmer for 5 minutes. Remove from heat.

In another pan melt three tablespoons of butter. Add in paprika and a teaspoon of dried mint and fry for a minute. Pour butter mixture over the soup and serve hot.

Greek Lemon Chicken Soup

Serves 4-5

Ingredients:

1.2 oz uncooked boneless, skinless chicken breast, diced

1/3 cup rice

2 cups chicken broth

1 cup water

1 onion, finely diced

2 raw eggs

3 tbsp olive oil

1/2 cup fresh lemon juice

1 tsp salt

1/2 tsp ground black pepper

1/2 cup finely cut parsley, to serve

Directions:

In a medium pot, heat the olive oil and sauté the onions until they are soft and translucent. Add the chicken broth, water, the washed rice and bring everything to a boil, then reduce heat. When the rice is almost done, add in the diced chicken breast. Let it cook for another 5 minutes, or until the chicken is cooked through.

In a small bowl, beat the eggs and lemon juice together. Pour two cups of broth slowly into the egg mixture, whisking constantly. When all the broth is incorporated, add this mixture back into the pot of chicken soup and stir well to blend. Do not boil any more. Season with salt and pepper and garnish with parsley. Serve hot.

Bean, Chicken and Sausage Soup

Serves 8

Ingredients:

10.5 oz Italian sausage

3 bacon strips, diced

2 cups chicken, cooked and diced

1 cup canned beans, rinsed and drained

1 big onion, chopped

2 garlic cloves, pressed

3 cups water

1 cup canned tomatoes, diced, undrained

1 bay leaf

1 tsp dried thyme

1 tsp savory

1/2 tsp dried basil

salt and pepper, to taste

Directions:

Cook the sausage, onion and bacon over medium heat until the sausage is no longer pink. Drain off the fat. Add the garlic and cook for a minute. Add the water, tomatoes and seasonings and bring to a boil.

Cover, reduce heat, and simmer for 30 minutes. Add chicken and beans. Simmer for 5 minutes more and serve.

Moroccan Chicken and Butternut Squash Soup

Serves 8

Ingredients:

3 skinless, boneless chicken thighs, cut into bite-sized pieces

1 big onion, chopped

1 zucchini, quartered lengthwise and sliced into 1/2-inch pieces

3 cups peeled butternut squash, cut in 1/2-inch pieces

2 tbsp tomato paste

4 cups chicken broth

1/3 cup uncooked couscous

1/2 tsp ground cumin

1/4 tsp ground cinnamon

1 tsp paprika

2 tbsp fresh basil, chopped

1 tbsp grated orange rind

3 tbsp olive oil

Directions:

Heat a soup pot over medium heat. Gently sauté onion, for 3-4 minutes, stirring occasionally. Add chicken pieces and cook for 5 minutes until chicken is brown on all sides. Add cumin, cinnamon and paprika and stir well. Add butternut squash and tomato paste; stir again. Add chicken broth and bring to a boil, then reduce heat and simmer for 10 minutes.

Stir in couscous, salt and zucchini pieces; cook until squash is tender. Remove pot from heat. Season with salt and pepper to taste. Stir in chopped basil and orange rind and serve.

Chicken Soup with Vermicelli

Serves 4

Ingredients:

1 whole chicken leg or 1/2 lb chicken breast

1/2 cup vermicelli

1 carrot, grated

4 cups water

3 cloves of garlic, sliced

1 tsp salt

1/2 tsp black pepper

1 egg, beaten

2 tbsp lemon juice

Directions:

Place the chicken in a pot and add 4 cups of water. Add 1 teaspoon salt and boil until the chicken is cooked. Take the chicken out of the pot, let it cool a little and cut it into bite size pieces.

Add carrot and garlic to the soup and bring it to a boil. Add vermicelli and chicken pieces. Reduce heat and simmer over medium heat for 8-10 minutes. When ready, let it cool for a while.

Mix the beaten egg and lemon juice in a bowl and slowly stir into the soup. Do not boil it again. Serve soup warm, seasoned with black pepper to taste.

Creamy Zucchini Soup

Serves 4

Ingredients:

1 onion, finely chopped

2 garlic cloves, pressed

1 cup vegetable broth

1 cup water

5 zucchinis, peeled, thinly sliced

1 big potato, chopped

1/4 cup fresh basil leaves

1 tsp sugar

1/2 cup yogurt, to serve

Parmesan cheese, to serve

Directions:

Heat oil in a saucepan over medium heat and sauté the onion and garlic, stirring, for 2-3 minutes or until soft. Add vegetable broth and water and bring to the boil, then reduce heat to medium-low. Add zucchinis, the potato, a teaspoon of sugar, and simmer, stirring occasionally, for 10 minutes or until the zucchinis are soft. Add basil and simmer for 2-3 minutes more.

Set aside to cool, then blend in batches and reheat. Serve with a dollop of yogurt and sprinkled with Parmesan cheese.

Broccoli, Zucchini and Blue Cheese Soup

Serves 6

Ingredients:

2 leeks, white part only, sliced

1 head broccoli, coarsely chopped

2 zucchinis, chopped

1 potato, chopped

2 cups vegetable broth

2 cups water

3 tbsp olive oil

3.5 oz blue cheese, crumbled

1/3 cup light cream

Directions:

Heat the oil in a large saucepan over medium heat. Sauté the leeks, stirring, for 5 minutes, or until soft. Add bite sized pieces of broccoli, zucchinis, potato, water, and broth and bring to a boil. Reduce heat to low and simmer, stirring occasionally, for 10 minutes, or until vegetables are just tender. Remove from heat and set aside for 5 minutes to cool slightly.

Transfer soup to a blender. Add the cheese and blend in batches until smooth. Return to the saucepan and place over low heat. Add cream and stir to combine. Season with salt and pepper to taste.

Beetroot and Carrot Soup

Serves 6

Ingredients:

4 beets, washed and peeled

2 carrots, peeled, chopped

2 potatoes, peeled, chopped

1 medium onion, chopped

2 cups vegetable broth

2 cups water

2 tbsp yogurt

2 tbsp olive oil

5-6 spring onions, finely cut, to serve

Directions:

Peel and chop the beets. Heat olive oil in a saucepan over medium-high heat and sauté onion and carrot until onion is tender. Add beets, potatoes, broth and water. Bring to the boil. Reduce heat to medium and simmer, partially covered, for 30-40 minutes, or until beets are tender. Cool slightly.

Blend soup in batches until smooth. Return it to pan over low heat and cook, stirring, for 4-5 minutes, or until heated through. Season with salt and pepper. Serve soup topped with yogurt and sprinkled with spring onions.

Pumpkin and Bell Pepper Soup

Serves 4

Ingredients:

1 medium leek, chopped

9 oz pumpkin, peeled, deseeded, cut into small cubes

1/2 small red pepper, chopped

1 can tomatoes, undrained, diced

1 cup vegetable broth

1/2 tsp cumin

salt and black pepper, to taste

Directions:

Heat the olive oil in a medium saucepan and sauté the leek for 4-5 minutes. Add the pumpkin and bell pepper and cook, stirring, for 5 minutes. Add tomatoes, broth, and cumin and bring to the boil. Cover, reduce heat to low and simmer, stirring occasionally, for 30 minutes, or until the vegetables are soft.

Season with salt and pepper and leave aside to cool. Blend in batches and reheat.

Moroccan Pumpkin Soup

Serves 6

Ingredients:

1 leek, white part only, thinly sliced

3 cloves garlic, finely chopped

1/2 tsp ground ginger

1/2 tsp ground cinnamon

1/2 tsp ground cumin

2 carrots, peeled, coarsely chopped

2 lb pumpkin, peeled, deseeded, diced

1/3 cup chickpeas

5 tbsp olive oil

juice of 1/2 lemon

1/2 cup finely cut parsley, to serve

Directions:

Heat the oil in a large deep saucepan and sauté the leek, garlic and 2 teaspoons of salt, stirring occasionally, until soft. Add cinnamon, ginger and cumin and stir. Add carrots, pumpkin and chickpeas. Stir well. Add 5 cups of water and bring to the boil, then reduce heat and simmer for 50 minutes, or until chick peas are soft. Remove from heat, add lemon juice and blend soup, in batches, until smooth.

Return the soup to the pan and cook, stirring, for 4-5 minutes, or until heated through. Serve topped with parsley.

Broccoli and Potato Soup

Serves 6

Ingredients:

2 lb broccoli, cut into florets

2 potatoes, chopped

1 big onion, chopped

3 garlic cloves, pressed

4 cups water

1 tbsp olive oil

¼ tsp ground nutmeg

Directions:

Heat oil in a large saucepan over medium-high heat. Add onion and garlic and sauté, stirring, for 3 minutes, or until soft.

Add broccoli, potato and 4 cups of cold water. Cover and bring to the boil, then reduce heat to low. Simmer, stirring, for 10-15 minutes, or until potato is tender. Remove from heat. Blend until smooth. Return to pan. Cook for 5 minutes or until heated through. Season with nutmeg and pepper before serving.

Creamy Potato Soup

Serves 8-10

Ingredients:

4-5 medium potatoes, cut into small cubes

2 carrots, chopped

1 zucchini, chopped

1 celery rib, chopped

3 cups water

3 tbsp olive oil

1 cup whole milk

1/2 tsp dried rosemary

salt, to taste

black pepper, to taste

1/2 cup finely cut parsley, to serve

Directions:

Heat the olive oil over medium heat and sauté the vegetables for 2-3 minutes. Pour 3 cups of water, add the rosemary and bring the soup to a boil, then lower heat and simmer until all the vegetables are tender.

Blend soup in a blender until smooth. Add a cup of warm milk and blend some more. Serve warm, seasoned with black pepper and parsley sprinkled over each serving.

Carrot and Chickpea Soup

Serves 4-5

Ingredients:

3-4 big carrots, chopped

1 leek, chopped

4 cups vegetable broth

1 cup canned chickpeas, undrained

1/2 cup orange juice

2 tbsp olive oil

1/2 tsp cumin

1/2 tsp ginger

4-5 tbsp yogurt, to serve

Directions:

Heat oil in a large saucepan over medium heat. Add leek and carrots and sauté until soft. Add orange juice, broth, chickpeas and spices. Bring to the boil.

Reduce heat to medium-low and simmer, covered, for 15 minutes. Blend soup until smooth, season with salt and pepper and return to pan. Cook over low heat, stirring, for 4-5 minutes, or until heated through. Pour in 4-5 bowls, top with yogurt and serve.

Spicy Carrot Soup

Serves 6-7

Ingredients:

10 carrots, peeled and chopped

2 medium onions, chopped

4-5 cups water

2 cloves garlic, minced

1 red chili pepper, finely chopped

1/2 cup finely cut cilantro

5 tbsp olive oil

salt and pepper, to taste

1/2 cup heavy cream

Directions:

Heat the olive oil in a large pot over medium heat and sauté the onions, carrots, garlic and chili pepper until tender. Add 4-5 cups of water and bring to a boil. Reduce heat to low and simmer for 30 minutes.

Transfer the soup to a blender or food processor and blend until smooth. Return to the pot and continue cooking for a few more minutes. Remove soup from heat and stir in the cream. Serve with cilantro sprinkled over each serving.

Lentil, Barley and Mushroom Soup

Serves 4

Ingredients*:*

2 medium leeks, trimmed, halved, sliced

10 white button mushrooms, sliced

3 garlic cloves, cut

2 bay leaves

2 cups canned tomatoes, chopped, undrained

3/4 cup red lentils

1/3 cup barley

3 tbsp olive oil

1 tsp paprika

1 tsp savory

1/2 tsp cumin

Directions:

Heat oil in a large saucepan over medium-high heat. Sauté leeks and mushrooms for 3-4 minutes or until softened. Add cumin, paprika, savory and tomatoes, lentils, barley and 5 cups cold water. Season with salt and pepper.

Cover and bring to the boil. Reduce heat to low. Simmer for 35-40 minutes, or until barley is tender.

Mushroom Soup

Serves 4

Ingredients:

15 white button mushrooms, chopped

1 onion, chopped

2 garlic cloves, pressed

1 tsp dried thyme

3 cups vegetable broth

salt and pepper, to taste

3 tbsp olive oil

Directions:

Sauté the onions and garlic in a large soup pot until transparent. Add thyme and mushrooms.

Cook for 10 minutes then add the vegetable broth and simmer for another 10-20 minutes. Blend, season, and serve.

Mediterranean Chickpea Soup

Serves 8-10

Ingredients:

2 cups canned chickpeas, drained

5-6 spring onions, finely cut

2 cloves garlic, pressed

1 cup canned tomatoes, diced

2 cups vegetable broth

3 tbsp olive oil

1 bay leaf

1/2 tsp rosemary

1/2 cup Parmesan cheese

Directions:

Sauté the onion and garlic in olive oil in a heavy soup pot. Add broth, chickpeas, tomatoes, bay leaf and rosemary.

Bring to boil, then reduce heath and simmer for 20 minutes. Remove from heat and serve sprinkled with Parmesan cheese.

French-style Vegetable Soup

Serves 6

Ingredients:

1 leek, thinly sliced

1 large zucchini, diced

1 cup green beans, cut

2 garlic cloves, cut

3 cups vegetable broth

1 cup canned tomatoes, chopped

3.5 oz vermicelli, broken into small pieces

3 tbsp olive oil

black pepper to taste

4 tbsp freshly grated Parmesan cheese

Directions:

Sauté the leek, zucchini, green beans and garlic for about 5 minutes. Add the vegetable broth. Stir in the tomatoes and bring to the boil then reduce heat.

Add black pepper to taste and simmer for 10 minutes, or until the vegetables are tender but still holding their shape. Stir in the vermicelli. Cover again and simmer for a further 5 minutes. Serve warm sprinkled with Parmesan cheese.

Moroccan Lentil Soup

Serves 10

Ingredients:

1 cup red lentils

1 cup canned chickpeas, drained

2 onions, chopped

2 cloves garlic, minced

1 cup canned tomatoes, chopped

1 cup canned white beans, drained

3 carrots, diced

3 celery ribs, diced

4 cups water

1 tsp ginger, grated

1 tsp ground cardamom

1/2 tsp ground cumin

3 tbsp olive oil

Directions:

In a large pot, sauté onions, garlic and ginger in olive oil for about 5 minutes. Add the water, lentils, chickpeas, white beans, tomatoes, carrots, celery, cardamom and cumin.

Bring to a boil for a few minutes then simmer for half an hour or longer, until the lentils are tender. Puree half the soup in a food processor or blender. Return the pureed soup to the pot, stir, and serve.

Minestrone

Serves 6-7

Ingredients:

¼ cabbage, chopped

2 carrots, chopped

1 celery rib, thinly sliced

1 small onion, chopped

2 garlic cloves, chopped

2 tbsp olive oil

2 cups water

1 cup canned tomatoes, diced, undrained

1 cup fresh spinach, torn

1/2 cup pasta, cooked

black pepper and salt, to taste

Directions:

Sauté the carrots, cabbage, celery, onion and garlic in oil for 5 minutes in a deep saucepan. Add water, tomatoes, and bring to a boil.

Reduce heat and simmer, uncovered, for 20 minutes, or until vegetables are tender. Stir in spinach, pasta, and season with black pepper and salt to taste.

Roasted Red Pepper Soup

Serves 6-7

Ingredients:

5-6 red peppers

1 large onion, chopped

2 garlic cloves, pressed

4 medium tomatoes, chopped

2 cups chicken broth

3 tbsp olive oil

2 bay leaves

Directions:

Grill the peppers or roast them in the oven at 400 F until the skins are a little burnt. Place the roasted peppers in a brown paper bag or a lidded container and leave covered for about 10 minutes. This makes it easier to peel them. Peel the skins and remove the seeds. Cut the peppers in small pieces.

Heat oil in a large saucepan over medium-high heat. Add onion and garlic and sauté, stirring, for 3 minutes, or until the onion has softened. Add the red peppers, bay leaves, tomato and simmer for 5 minutes.

Add in chicken broth. Season with black pepper. Bring to the boil then reduce heat and simmer for 20 minutes. Set aside to cool slightly. Blend, in batches, until smooth and serve.

Leek, Rice and Potato Soup

Serves 6

Ingredients:

1/3 cup rice

4 cups of water

2-3 potatoes, diced

1 small onion, cut

1 leek halved lengthwise and finely cut

3 tbsp olive oil

lemon juice, to serve

Directions:

Heat a soup pot over medium heat. Add olive oil and onion and sauté for 2 minutes. Add leeks and potatoes, stir, and cook for a few minutes more. Add three cups of water, bring to a boil, reduce heat and simmer for 5 minutes. Add in the very well washed rice and simmer for 15 minutes. Serve with lemon juice to taste.

Spinach, Nettle and Feta Cheese Soup

Serves 6

Ingredients:

1 lb frozen spinach, thawed

13 oz nettles, young top shoots

3.5 oz feta cheese

1 large onion or 4-5 scallions

2 -3 tbsp light cream

3-4 tbsp olive oil

¼ cup white rice

1-2 garlic cloves, chopped

2 cups water

black pepper, to taste

salt, to taste

Directions:

Clean the young nettles, wash and cook them in slightly salted water. Drain, rinse, drain again, chop them and leave aside.

Heat the oil in a soup pot, add the onion, garlic and paprika and sauté for a few minutes, stirring constantly. Remove from heat. Add the spinach and nettles. Add about 4 cups of hot water and season with salt and pepper. Bring back to the boil, then reduce heat and simmer for around 30 minutes. In the meantime crumble the cheese with a fork. When the soup is ready, stir in the crumbled feta cheese and the cream. Serve hot.

Gazpacho

Serves 6-7

Ingredients:

2.25 lb tomatoes, peeled and halved

1 onion, sliced

1 green pepper, sliced

1 big cucumber, peeled and sliced

2 garlic cloves

4 tbsp olive oil

1 tbsp apple vinegar

salt, to taste

to garnish

1/2 onion, chopped

1 green pepper, chopped

1 cucumber, chopped

Directions:

Place the tomatoes, garlic, onion, green pepper, cucumber, salt, olive oil and vinegar in a blender or food processor and puree until smooth, adding small amounts of cold water, if needed, to achieve desired consistency.

Serve the gazpacho chilled with the chopped onion, green pepper and cucumber.

Main Dish Recipes

Moroccan Beef Couscous

Serves 6

Ingredients:

2 lbs stewing beef

1 onion, cut

1/2 cup canned chickpeas, drained

2 zucchinis, cut

1/2 cup green peas

3 potatoes, peeled and cut

2 carrots, halved

2 red peppers, cut

1/2 cup black olives, pitted

3 tbsp tomato paste

3 cups water

1 tsp cumin

1 tsp paprika

1 bunch parsley

5 tbsp olive oil

2 cups couscous

2 cups water

Directions:

Heat a large saucepan over medium-high heat. Brown the beef in olive oil. Add in the onion and sauté, stirring, for 2-3 minutes. Stir in cumin, paprika and water and bring to a boil. Reduce heat, cover and simmer for an hour then add in all remaining vegetables, olives, and the tomato paste.

Tie the parsley into a bouquet and place it on top of everything. Cover the pot and simmer for 30 minutes or until the meat is done and the vegetables are tender. Discard the parsley bouquet.

Boil two cups of water and pour it over the couscous. Set aside for 3-4 minutes then fluff gently with a fork.

Serve couscous with meat and vegetables on top and stew sauce in a separate bowl.

Spanish Marinated Skewers

Serves 4

Ingredients:

2 lbs beef, cut into 1 inch cubes

1 onion, chopped

4 garlic cloves, chopped

2 tbsp parsley, chopped

1 tbsp paprika

1/2 cup olive oil

1/3 cup dry red wine

12 small white button mushrooms, whole

1 tbsp paprika

2 tbsp red wine vinegar

1/2 cup olive oil

1 tbsp fresh rosemary leaves

Directions:

Place the beef cubes in a bowl together with the chopped onion and garlic. Add wine, paprika, parsley and olive oil. Mix thoroughly and marinate for at least an hour.

Thread beef onto skewers dividing the cubes with mushrooms. Grill on a hot barbecue, turning, until cooked through.

Prepare the dressing by combining paprika, vinegar, oil and rosemary.

Place skewers on plates and drizzle dressing on top. Serve with fresh vegetable salad or rice.

Italian Roast Beef

Serves 6

Ingredients:

5 lb roast beef round

6 garlic cloves, sliced

4 onions, sliced

6 carrots, cut into rounds

4 celery ribs, cut into thick pieces

2 bay leaves

1 tbsp finely chopped rosemary

1/4 cup tomato paste

1 cup dry white wine

1/4 tsp black pepper

1/3 cup dried basil

1/3 cup dried oregano

1/2 cup olive oil

Directions:

Preheat oven to 300 F. Combine all the spice in a bowl. Poke holes all over the roast and stick some garlic into the holes.

Heat olive oil, in a large ovenproof dish and seal the meat on all sides then transfer it to a plate. Coat meat with the spice mix and drizzle olive oil on top.

Arrange the roast beef in the middle of the baking dish. Add in onions, bay leaves, carrots, celery, rosemary, wine and tomato paste.

Bake on lowest rack for approximately 2 hours, uncovered, until the internal temperature reaches 140 F (160 F for well done). Remove roast beef from oven and set aside to cool, for about 20-30 minutes. Use for sandwiches or serve with gravy.

Beef and Broccoli Stew

Serves 4

Ingredients:

1/2 lb flank steak, cut in strips

3 cups broccoli florets

1 onion, chopped

5-6 white button mushrooms, chopped

1 cup beef broth

1/3 cup cashew nuts

1 tsp cornstarch

3 tbsp olive oil

2 tbsp soy sauce

1 tbsp honey

1 tsp lemon zest

1 tsp grated ginger

Directions:

Place meat in the freezer for 20 minutes then cut it in thin slices. In a mixing bowl, combine steak, soy sauce, honey, lemon zest and ginger. Stir to coat well and set aside for 30 minutes.

Quickly stir fry broccoli, onion, mushrooms and cashews in olive oil, over high heat, for 2-3 minutes. Transfer to a warm bowl. Stir fry steak about 2-3 minutes until cooked through. Stir in vegetables. Dilute cornstarch into beef broth and add it to the meat mixture. Stir until thickened. Serve over noodles or rice.

Italian Beef Stew

Serves 4

Ingredients:

1.5 lbs stewing beef

1 egg

9 oz feta cheese

2 tbsp water

5-6 roasted red peppers

2/3 cup fresh basil leaves, chopped

Directions:

Whisk egg and water in a bowl. Season with salt and pepper. In a second bowl, combine breadcrumbs and half of the cheese. Cut meat into 8-9 equal pieces. Dip each piece into the egg mixture, then in the breadcrumb mixture. Press lightly to coat. Heat 2 tablespoons of olive oil in a large skillet and and cook the beef in batches for 5-6 minutes. Set aside in a plate, covered.

Prepare the sauce by blending the roasted and peeled red peppers with the remaining cheese. Blend until almost smooth. Clean the skillet and cook the pepper mixture until heated through. Stir in half the basil leaves. Add the beef pieces and stir. Set aside for a few minutes and serve sprinkled with the remaining basil.

Beef Stew with Quince

Serves 6-8

Ingredients:

2 lbs chuck roast, trimmed of fat and cut into 2 inch pieces

2 onions, chopped

2-3 tomatoes, pureed

1-2 bay leaves

1 cinnamon stick

1 cup dry white wine

3 quinces, peeled, cored and cubed

5-6 prunes

1 tsp paprika

1 tsp salt

1/2 tsp black pepper

1 tbsp honey

6 tbsp olive oil

Directions:

Heat half the olive oil in a large pot over medium-high heat. Seal the meat in batches, then set it aside in a plate. Sauté the onions for 6-8 minutes. Add the meat back to the pot. Add the wine, bay leaves, cinnamon, tomato puree, salt, pepper, and enough water to cover the meat. Stir and bring the pot to a simmer.

Heat remaining olive oil in a skillet and sauté the quince for 3-4 minutes until the edges start to caramelize. Add the quince to the stew pot along with the prunes and the honey. Stir, cover, and simmer for two hours over low heat. Stir occasionally and make sure there is enough liquid in the pot. If it looks dry, add some water. Before serving discard the bay leaves and cinnamon stick.

Spanish Beef Stew

2 lbs stewing beef

1 tbsp flour

1 cup beef broth

1/2 cup dry red wine

3 leeks, chopped

6 garlic cloves, halved

2 onions, chopped

1 carrot, sliced

1 celery rib, chopped

1 tomato, chopped

2 oz cooking chocolate

1/4 tsp cinnamon

1/4 cup olive oil

salt and pepper, to taste

Directions:

Heat the olive oil in a large pot. Seal the stewing meat for 3-4 minutes, or until well browned on all sides. Add the flour and stir. Add the wine and stir. Cook for 2-3 minutes. Add the garlic, onions, tomatoes, carrot, celery and leaks to the pot and stir to combine.

Add chocolate and beef broth, stir, and bring to a boil. Reduce heat, cover partially, and simmer for an hour and a half, or until the meat is cooked through.

Mediterranean Beef Casserole

Serves 6

Ingredients:

2 lb lean steak, cut into large pieces

3 onions, sliced

4 garlic cloves, cut

2 red peppers, cut

1 green pepper, cut

1 zucchini, cut

3 tomatoes, quartered

2 tbsp tomato paste or purée

1/2 cup green olives, pitted

1/2 cup dry red wine

1/2 cup of water

1 tsp dry oregano

salt and black pepper, to taste

Directions:

Heat olive oil in a deep baking dish and seal the beef. Add vegetables and stir.

Dilute the tomato paste in half a cup of water and pour it over the meat mixture together with the wine. Season well and bake, covered, in a preheated to 350 F oven, for one hour.

Mediterranean Beef and Brown Rice Stew

Serves 4

Ingredients:

1 lb stewing beef

1 onion, chopped

2 garlic cloves, pressed

14 oz canned artichoke hearts, drained, chopped

5-6 white button mushrooms, cut

2 cups canned tomatoes, diced, undrained

1 tbsp balsamic vinegar

1 tbsp drained capers

1 tsp basil

1 tsp salt

1 tsp sugar

2 cups brown rice

3 tbsp olive oil

black pepper, to taste

1/2 cup Parmesan cheese, grated

Directions:

Heat olive oil in a deep pot and seal the beef pieces. Add in onion and garlic and cook for 2-3 minutes. Add all the other vegetables and seasonings and bring to the boil. Reduce heat and simmer, covered, for an hour. Uncover and simmer for 5 more minutes.

Prepare brown rice as directed on package. Serve it with beef mixture on top and sprinkled with Parmesan cheese.

Beef and Onion Stew

Serves 6

Ingredients:

2 lbs lean beef, cubed

3 lbs shallots, peeled

5 garlic cloves, peeled, whole

3 tbsp tomato paste

1 bay leaves

1/4 cup of olive oil

3 tbsp red wine vinegar

1 tsp salt

Directions:

Heat a stew pot and brown the meat in olive oil. Add remaining ingredients and enough water to cover everything.

Bring to a boil. Reduce heat to low, cover, and simmer for 1-2 hours, stirring occasionally, until beef is cooked through.

Beef Stew with Green Peas

Serves 6

Ingredients:

2 lbs stewing beef

2 bags(10 oz each) frozen green peas

1 onion, diced

3-4 garlic cloves, cut

2 carrots, chopped

1/3 cups olive oil

1 cup water

1 tsp salt

1 tbsp paprika

1/2 cup fresh dill, finely chopped

1 cup yogurt (optional)

Directions:

Season the meat pieces with salt and black pepper. Heat the olive oil in a large stewing pot and sauté onion and meat until the meat is well browned. Add paprika, carrots, garlic, frozen green peas and water.

Bring to the boil, then reduce heat; cover and simmer for an hour. Serve sprinkled with fresh dill and a dollop of yogurt.

Potato Beef Stew

Serves 6

Ingredients:

2 lbs stewing beef

5 potatoes, cubed

2 carrots, chopped

1 onion, sliced

3 garlic cloves, pressed

4 tbsp tomato paste or purée

1 cup water

3 tbsp olive oil

1 tsp paprika

1/2 tsp savory

1 tsp salt

1/2 tsp ground black pepper

1/2 cup parsley leaves, chopped, to serve

Directions:

Heat olive oil in a large soup pot over medium-high heat and sauté the beef pieces for 3-4 minutes until well sealed. Add carrots, onion and garlic and sauté for 3 more minutes, stirring. Add paprika and savory and stir.

Dissolve the tomato paste in a cup of water and pour over the meat. Add salt and black pepper and stir again. Bring to the boil, then reduce heat and simmer for 40 minutes. Add potatoes and simmer for 20 more minutes, or until potatoes are tender. Sprinkle with chopped parsley and serve hot.

Beef with Mushrooms

Serves 4

Ingredients:

1 lb stewing beef

14-15 white button mushrooms, sliced

2 leeks, chopped

4 garlic cloves, sliced

3 tbsp olive oil

2 tbsp tomato paste or purée

1/2 cup water

1/2 cup dry red wine

1 tsp paprika

1 tsp dried thyme

1 tsp salt

1 tsp sugar

black pepper, to taste

Directions:

Heat the olive oil in a large pot and seal the beef pieces very well. Add in the leeks, garlic and white wine and cook over low heat until the beef pieces are tender. Add sugar, paprika, thyme, salt and pepper and stir.

Dilute the tomato paste in half a cup of hot water. Pour it over the meat, stir and add the mushrooms. Cover and simmer, stirring from time to time, over medium-low heat for 40 minutes. Uncover and simmer some more until the liquid has evaporated. Serve over rice or pasta.

Beef and Spinach Stew

Serves 6

Ingredients:

1 lb stewing beef

10 oz frozen spinach or 6 cups fresh spinach leaves, cut

1 onion, chopped

1 carrot, chopped

2-3 white button mushrooms, cut

3 garlic cloves, pressed

1 cup beef broth

1/2 cup canned tomatoes, drained

4 tbsp olive oil

6 oz butter

1 tbsp paprika

salt and pepper, to taste

Directions:

In a large stew pot, heat the butter and olive oil and seal the beef pieces. Add onion, carrot, mushrooms and garlic and sauté for a few minutes. Add paprika, beef broth and bring to the boil then reduce heat and simmer, covered, for 30-40 minutes.

Add tomatoes and spinach. Stir and simmer, uncovered, for 10 minutes. Serve over rice or couscous.

Chickpeas with Beef

Serves 6

Ingredients:

1 lb lean beef meat, cubed

2 onions, chopped

2 cups canned chickpeas, drained

1 red bell pepper, chopped

3 tbsp olive oil

1 tbsp tomato paste

1 tsp paprika

1 tsp cumin

salt, to taste

1 cup water

Directions:

Heat olive oil in a large pot and seal cubed meat until well browned. Add onions, red pepper, paprika and cumin and sauté for 2-3 minutes over medium heat. Dilute tomato paste in a cup of water and pour over the meat.

Bring to the boil, reduce heat and simmer until the meat is done. Add the chickpeas into the pot. Season with salt and black pepper to the taste and simmer, uncovered, for 10 more minutes. Serve sprinkled with parsley, over rice pilaf.

Beef and Okra Stew

Serves 6

Ingredients:

1 lb stewing beef

1 lb frozen okra

1 onion, chopped

3 garlic cloves, pressed

1 cup canned tomatoes, diced

3 tbsp tomato purée

1/2 tsp cumin

1 cup water

4 tbsp olive oil

salt and pepper, to taste

Directions:

In a large saucepan, heat olive oil and seal meat. Add onions and garlic and sauté, stirring for 2-3 minutes. Add tomatoes, cumin, salt and pepper. Add water and tomato purée. Stir and combine well.

Add okra and bring to a boil, then reduce heat to low and simmer, covered, for an hour, or until meat is tender and done. Uncover and simmer for five more minutes. Serve with white rice or couscous.

Mixed Vegetables with Beef

Serves 6-8

Ingredients:

2 lbs stewing beef

2 eggplants, cubed

5 small potatoes, halved

1 zucchini, cubed

2 red peppers, cut

1 cup frozen okra

1 onion, sliced

4 garlic cloves, cut

3 tomatoes, diced

1 cup parsley leaves, chopped

1/4 cup olive oil

1 tsp paprika

salt, to taste

black pepper, to taste

Directions:

Sprinkle the eggplant pieces with salt and set aside in a strainer for 15 minutes. Wash the salt and the excess juices and pat dry the eggplant pieces.

Heat the olive oil in a large pot and sauté the beef pieces for a few minutes until well browned. Add in the vegetables, stirring. Add paprika, salt and pepper and stir very well. Transfer the meat and vegetables to an ovenproof dish and bake in a preheated to 305 F oven for an hour. Sprinkle with parsley and serve.

Spinach with Ground Beef

Serves 4

Ingredients:

10 oz ground beef

6 cups fresh spinach, chopped

1 tomato, cubed

1 onion, finely chopped

1/3 cup rice

4 tbsp olive oil

1 tsp paprika

salt, to taste

black pepper, to taste

Directions:

Heat the olive oil in a large pot and sauté the onion for about 2-3 minutes. Add the ground beef, paprika, salt and black pepper and stir. Cook until the the ground beef turns brown.

Add the rice, tomato, and stir again. Simmer, covered, for 20 minutes. Add the spinach and cook until it wilts. Serve with a dollop of yogurt.

Ground Beef and Chickpea Casserole

Serves 6

Ingredients:

1 lb ground beef

1 onion, chopped

2 garlic cloves, pressed

1 can chickpeas, drained

1 can sweet corn, drained

1 can tomato sauce

1/2 cup water

2 bay leaves

1 tsp dried oregano

1/2 tsp salt

1/2 tsp cumin

3 tbsp olive oil

black pepper, to taste

Directions:

Heat the olive oil in a casserole over medium-high heat. Add the onion and sauté for 4-5 minutes. Add garlic and sauté a minute more. Add in the ground beef and cook for 5 minutes, stirring, until browned.

Add the cumin and bay leaves, the tomatoes, corn and chickpeas. Bring everything to the boil, then reduce heat and simmer for 20 minutes, or until the beef is cooked through. Remove the bay leaves and serve over rice or couscous.

Ground Beef and Rice Stuffed Peppers

Serves 6

Ingredients*:*

8 red or green bell peppers, cored and seeded

2 lbs ground beef

1/4 cup rice, washed and drained

1 onion, finely cut

1 tomato, grated

1/2 cup finely cut parsley

3 tbsp olive oil

1 tbsp paprika

Directions:

Heat the oil and sauté the onion for 2-3 minutes. Remove from heat. Add paprika, ground beef, rice, tomato, and season with salt and pepper. Combine very well and stuff each pepper with the mixture using a spoon. Every pepper should be 3/4 full.

Arrange the peppers in a deep ovenproof dish and top up with warm water to half fill the dish. Cover and bake for about 40-50 minutes at 350 F. Serve with yogurt.

Stuffed Cabbage Leaves with Ground Beef and Rice

Serves 8

Ingredients:

1 lb ground beef

20-30 medium sized pickled cabbage leaves

1 onion, diced

1 leek, finely cut

1/2 cup white rice

2 tsp tomato paste

2 tsp paprika

1 tsp dried mint

1/2 tsp black pepper

1/3 cup olive oil

salt to taste

Directions:

Sauté the onion and leek in the oil for about 2-3 minutes. Remove from heat and add the beef, tomato paste, paprika, mint, black pepper and the washed and drained rice. Add salt only if the cabbage leaves are not too salty. Mix everything very well.

In a large pot place a few cabbage leaves on the base. Place a cabbage leaf on a large plate with the thickest part closest to you. Spoon 1-2 teaspoons of the meat mixture and fold over each edge to create a tight sausage-like parcel. Place in the pot in two or three layers.

Cover with a few cabbage leaves and pour over some boiling water so that the water level remains lower than the top layer of cabbage leaves. Top with a small dish upside down to prevent scattering.

Bring to the boil, then lower the heat and cook for around an hour.

Meatballs with Parsley Sauce

Serves 6-8

Ingredients:

2 lbs lean ground beef

4 slices bacon, finely cut

1 onion, finely chopped

2 garlic cloves, finely chopped

1/2 cup parsley leaves, very finely cut

1/2 cup breadcrumbs, for coating

1 cup olive oil for frying

for the sauce:

1 cup breadcrumbs

3 cups beef broth

1 cup parsley leaves, finely cut

1/4 cup walnuts, crushed

Directions:

Place the ground beef, onion, garlic, parsley and bacon in a large bowl and mix with hands. Form into meatballs.

Heat olive oil in a large frying pan. Put the breadcrumbs on a plate and coat each meatball. Fry meatballs in the frying pan in batches, turning, until the meat is cooked through. When ready place them on a paper towel to absorb the extra oil.

Put the broth, breadcrumbs and a cup of parsley leaves into a large pot. Stir and bring to a boil. Add the nuts and stir. Simmer for about 5 minutes. Add the meatballs to the parsley sauce. Serve over rice or with potato mash.

Meatballs in Tomato Sauce

Serves 6

Ingredients:

2 lbs ground beef

2 onions, grated

1 carrot, chopped

2 garlic cloves, cut

3-4 white button mushrooms, sliced

1 cup breadcrumbs

1/3 cup parsley leaves, finely chopped, for the meatballs

3 cups canned tomatoes, diced

1/2 cup chicken broth

1/2 cup parsley leaves, to serve

Directions:

Combine ground beef, finely cut onion, breadcrumbs, parsley, salt and pepper in a large bowl. Roll tablespoonfuls of mince mixture into balls. Place meatballs on a tray lined with baking paper and set aside.

Heat oil in a deep frying pan. Sauté finely cut onion, carrot and garlic for 2-3 minutes, stirring. Add mushrooms and stir again. Add tomatoes and broth and bring slowly to the boil over medium heat. Drop meatballs into the tomato mixture. Reduce heat to low and simmer, uncovered, for 30 minutes or until the meatballs are cooked through.

Sprinkle with parsley, set aside for 5 minutes and serve.

Mediterranean Meatloaf

Serves 4

Ingredients:

1 lb ground beef

1/3 cup brown rice

1 small red onion, grated

1 carrot, peeled, grated

3 oz feta cheese, crumbled

2 tbsp tomato sauce

1 egg, lightly beaten

2 tbsp basil leaves, finely cut

1 zucchini, thinly sliced

1 cup cherry tomatoes

1 garlic clove, pressed

2-3 tbsp olive oil

Directions:

Cook rice following package directions. Set aside to cool.

Preheat oven to 350 F. Grease the base and sides of a 8 x 4 x 2.5 inch loaf pan or line it with baking paper.

Combine rice, onion, ground beef, carrot, feta, sauce, egg and basil in a bowl. Mix well and press into prepared pan. Place zucchini, tomatoes and garlic in a bowl and toss them in olive oil then arrange over meatloaf. Bake for 40-50 minutes in a preheated to 350 F oven or until meatloaf is firm.

Set aside for 10 minutes, slice and serve.

Homemade Lasagna

Serves 9-10

Ingredients:

1.5 lbs lean ground beef

10 oz pancetta or bacon, cut into 1/4-inch pieces

1 onion, finely chopped

2 carrots, chopped

2 celery ribs, chopped

3 garlic cloves, pressed

1/2 cup dry white wine

1/2 cup chicken broth

2 cups canned tomatoes, diced

3 tbsp tomato paste

1 tbsp dried basil

1/3 cup parsley

1/2 tsp ground black pepper

1 tsp paprika

2 cups mozzarella cheese, shredded

1 cup Parmesan cheese, shredded

12 no-cook lasagna noodles

Directions:

Heat olive oil in a large pot and cook ground beef, pancetta, onion, carrots, celery, and garlic over medium-high heat until ground meat turns brown. Bring to a simmer and cook, uncovered, until liquid is nearly evaporated. Stir in wine and beef broth and continue simmering until liquid evaporates. Add in paprika, tomatoes, tomato paste, parsley, black pepper and salt.

Combine mozzarella and Parmesan cheese in a medium bowl.

Spread one-third of the meat sauce over the bottom of an ungreased 13x9x2-inch baking dish. Cover with one-fourth of the cheese mixture. Layer noodles.

Repeat layering meat sauce, cheese mixture, and noodles two more times. Cover the dish with foil and bake in a preheated to 350 F oven for 40 minutes. Sprinkle with remaining cheese mixture and bake, uncovered, about 5 more minutes until the cheese turns gold. Set aside for 10 minutes and serve.

Beef and Spinach Lasagna

Serves 8-10

Ingredients:

1 lb lean ground beef

10 oz frozen spinach

1 onion, chopped

2 cups canned tomatoes

4 garlic cloves, pressed

1 tsp dried basil

1 tsp dried oregano

2 cups ricotta cheese

2 cups mozzarella cheese, shredded

12 no-cook lasagna noodles

Directions:

In a large skillet, sauté onion for a few minutes. Add beef and cook over medium heat until meat is no longer pink. Add in the tomatoes, garlic, basil and oregano. Simmer for 10 minutes. In a large bowl, combine the thawed spinach with half the ricotta and mozzarella cheese.

Spread one-third of the meat sauce over the bottom of an ungreased 13x9x2-inch baking dish. Sprinkle with one-fourth of the spinach -cheese mixture. Top with noodles. Repeat layering meat sauce, spinach mixture, and noodles two more times.

Cover dish with foil. Bake for 40 minutes in a preheated to 350 F oven. Sprinkle with the remaining cheese mixture. Bake, uncovered, about 5 minutes, until cheese turns golden. Let stand for at least 10 minutes before serving.

Ground Beef Pasta with Yogurt Sauce

Serves 5

Ingredients:

2 cups small pasta

1 lb ground beef

1 onion, chopped

2 tbsp butter

2 tbsp olive oil

salt and black pepper, to taste

for the sauce:

11/2 cup yogurt, room temperature

5 garlic cloves, pressed

Directions:

Prepare the sauce by mixing well yogurt and garlic.

Sauté the onion in olive oil, for 2-3 minutes, over medium heat. Add the ground beef and cook for 10 minutes, or until the meat is cooked through.

Cook pasta as described on package instructions. Drain and set aside. Melt the butter in a large pot and toss the pasta in it.

Serve pasta, topped with the cooked ground beef and generously covered with the yogurt sauce.

Baked Ground Beef Pasta

Serves 6

Ingredients:

2 cups large pasta

1 lb ground beef

2 onions, finely chopped

4 garlic cloves, chopped

3-4 white button mushrooms, chopped

5-6 pickled gherkins, chopped

1 cup canned tomatoes, drained

1 tsp paprika

1 tsp dry basil

salt and black pepper, to taste

1/2 cup parsley leaves, chopped

1 cup mozzarella cheese, grated

1 egg, whisked

Directions:

Prepare pasta according to package directions. Drain and place in an ovenproof dish.

Heat olive oil in a large pot and sauté onion until transparent. Add ground beef, mushrooms, garlic and tomatoes, stir and cook on low heat for about 15 minutes.

When the meat is almost done, add the gherkins, the parsley and toss everything with the pasta. Whisk the egg with mozzarella cheese and spread all over the pasta equally. Bake in a preheated to 350 F oven for 10 minutes, or until the cheese turns golden.

Mediterranean Chicken Stew

Serves 4

Ingredients:

4 chicken breast halves

1 big onion, sliced

1 red bell pepper, thinly sliced

2 cups tomato pasta sauce

1/2 cup black olives, pitted

1/2 green olives, pitted

1/3 cup Parmesan cheese

¼ cup chopped parsley

3 tbsp olive oil

Directions:

Heat the oil in a large, deep, frying pan over medium-high heat. Cook chicken, turning, for 4 to 5 minutes or until golden. Transfer to a plate.

Sauté onion and bell pepper, stirring, for 3 to 4 minutes, or until onion has softened. Return chicken to pan. Add pasta sauce and olives. Season with salt and pepper. Cover and bring to the boil.

Reduce heat to low and simmer for 30 to 35 minutes or until the chicken is cooked through. Sprinkle with Parmesan cheese, parsley and serve.

Chicken Potato Casserole

Serves 4

Ingredients:

4 skinless, boneless chicken breast halves

12 oz baby potatoes

1 onion, sliced

2 carrots, cut

1 red bell pepper, halved, deseeded, cut

1 zucchini, cut

4 garlic cloves, thinly sliced

1 cup water

3 tbsp olive oil

1 tsp oregano

Directions:

Preheat oven to 350 F. Heat oil in a non stick frying pan over medium heat. Cook half the chicken, turning occasionally, for 5 minutes or until brown all over. Set aside. Repeat with remaining chicken.

Peel the potatoes and cut into quarters, lengthwise. Peel and cut the carrots and the zucchini. Cut the onion and the pepper. Transfer chicken to a roasting pan, add vegetables, on and around the chicken.

Add dry oregano, garlic and water, distributing evenly across the pan. Bake, uncovered, at 350 F for one hour. Half way through stir gently. If needed, add a little more water.

Chicken and Onion Stew

Serves 4

Ingredients:

4 chicken breast halves

4-5 big onions, thinly sliced

1/2 cup black olives, pitted

4 tbsp olive oil

1 tsp thyme

1 tsp turmeric

salt and black pepper to taste

1/4 cup parsley leaves, chopped, to serve

Directions:

Heat the oil in a large, deep, frying pan over medium-high heat. Cook chicken, turning, for 4 to 5 minutes or until golden. Transfer to a plate.

Sauté thinly sliced onions, stirring gently, for 5 minutes, until soft. Add olives, thyme, turmeric, salt and pepper to taste. Return chicken to pan.

Cover and bring to the boil. Reduce heat to low and simmer for 35 minutes, or until chicken is cooked through. Sprinkle with parsley and serve.

Chicken and Mushrooms

Serves 4

Ingredients:

4 chicken breast halves, diced

14-15 white button mushrooms, sliced

6-7 spring onions, chopped

1/2 cup light cream

4 tbsp olive oil

1 tsp thyme

salt and black pepper, to taste

Directions:

Heat oil in a large, deep, frying pan over medium-high heat. Cook chicken, stirring, for 4-5 minutes or until golden. Add spring onions, mushrooms, salt and pepper and stir.

Cover and bring to the boil. Reduce heat to low and simmer for 20 minutes then stir in cream. Simmer for 5 more minutes and serve.

Mediterranean Chicken Drumstick Casserole

Serves 4

*Ingredients***:**

8 chicken drumsticks

1 leek, trimmed, thinly sliced

2 garlic cloves, pressed

1 cup canned tomatoes

1 tsp dry rosemary

1 cup canned chickpeas, drained and rinsed

cooked orzo or couscous, to serve

Directions:

Preheat oven to 350 F. Heat the oil in a non stick frying pan over medium heat. Add half the chicken and cook, turning occasionally, for 5 minutes or until brown all over. Transfer chicken to a big baking dish. Repeat with the remaining chicken.

Add leek and garlic to the pan and cook, stirring, for 3 minutes or until soft. Add tomatoes, chickpeas, thyme and rosemary, and bring to the boil. Remove from heat. Pour over the chicken.

Cover and bake for 40 minutes or until chicken is tender. Season with salt and pepper. Serve with orzo or couscous.

Greek Chicken Casserole

Serves 4

Ingredients:

4 skinless, boneless chicken breast halves or 8 tights

2 lb potatoes, cubed

1/2 lb green beans, trimmed and cut in 1 inch pieces

1 big onion, chopped

2 cups diced, canned tomatoes, undrained

5 cloves garlic, minced

1/4 cup water

1/2 cup feta cheese, crumbled

salt and black pepper, to taste

Directions:

Preheat oven to 350 F. Heat oil in a large baking dish over medium heat. Add onion and sauté for 2 minutes. Add thyme, black pepper and garlic and sauté for another minute. Add potatoes and sauté for 2-3 minutes, or until they begin to brown. Stir in beans, water, and tomatoes.

Remove from heat. Arrange chicken pieces into the vegetables, sprinkle with salt and pepper and top with feta. Cover and bake for 40 minutes, stirring gently halfway through.

Serve the vegetable mixture onto a plate, underneath or beside the chicken.

Hunter Style Chicken

Serves 4-6

Ingredients:

1 chicken (3-4 lbs), cut into pieces

2 tbsp olive oil

2 medium onions, thinly sliced

1 red bell pepper, cut

6-7 white button mushrooms, sliced

2 cups canned tomatoes, diced and drained

3 garlic cloves, thinly sliced

salt and freshly ground pepper

1/3 cup white wine

1/2 cup parsley leaves, finely cut

1 tsp sugar

Directions:

Rinse chicken pieces and pat dry. Heat olive oil in a large skillet on medium heat. Working in batches cook the chicken pieces until nicely browned, 5-6 minutes, then turn over and brown the other side. Transfer chicken to a bowl, set aside. Drain off all of the rendered fat. Add 2 tablespoons of olive oil and sauté the sliced onions and bell pepper for a few minutes. Add the mushrooms and cook some more until onion is translucent. Add garlic and cook a minute more.

Add wine and simmer until liquid is reduced by half. Add tomatoes and a teaspoon of sugar and stir. Place the chicken pieces on top of the tomatoes and onions, skin side up. Lower the heat and cover the skillet with the lid slightly ajar.

Simmer the chicken for about 40 minutes, turning from time to time, until meat is almost falling off the bones. Sprinkle with parsley, set aside for 3-4 minutes and serve.

Chicken Kofta

Serves 4

Ingredients:

1 lb ground chicken meat

1 onion, grated

1 egg, lightly whisked

1/3 cup breadcrumbs

3 tbsp chopped parsley leaves

1 tbs freshly ground ginger

1/2 tsp ground cinnamon

1/2 tsp ground nutmeg

2 tbsp olive oil

1 cup chicken broth

1 tsp brown sugar

1 tbsp lemon juice

Directions:

Preheat oven to 350 F. Line a baking tray with baking paper.

Place the ground chicken, onion, egg, breadcrumbs, chopped parsley, cinnamon, nutmeg and half the ginger in a bowl with a teaspoon salt. Mix with your hands until well combined. Using damp hands, roll mixture into walnut-sized balls, then place them on a tray in a single layer and bake for 15 minutes, until light golden.

Heat oil in a deep frying pan over medium heat. Add remaining ginger and stir for 1 minute until fragrant. Add tomatoes and cook for 2 minutes. Add broth and sugar. Bring to a boil, then reduce heat to medium low and simmer for 5 minutes. Add kofta and simmer for 20 minutes until kofta are cooked through and sauce has thickened. Serve kofta with rice, orzo or couscous garnished with extra parsley.

Roasted Chicken with Sumac

Serves 4

Ingredients:

1 whole chicken (3-4 lbs)

2 tbsp olive oil

2 garlic cloves, pressed

1 tbsp sumac

1 tsp lemon zest

1 tbsp lemon juice

1/2 cup fresh cilantro leaves, to serve

Directions:

Combine oil, garlic, sumac, lemon rind and lemon juice in a bowl. Rub mixture over chicken. Cover and marinate for 2 hours if time permits. Roast chicken in an ovenproof dish, covered, for 1 1/2 hours.

Uncover and roast for 20 minutes more, or until cooked through. Cut chicken into large pieces and serve sprinkled with cilantro and garnished with vegetable salads.

Chicken with Almonds and Prunes

Serves 4

Ingredients:

1.5 lb chicken thigh fillets, trimmed

1/2 cup fresh orange juice

2 tbsp honey

1/3 cup white wine

1/2 cup pitted prunes

2 tbsp blanched almonds

2 tbsp raisins or sultanas

1 tsp ground cinnamon

salt and ground black pepper

1 tbsp fresh parsley leaves, chopped

couscous (to serve)

Directions:

Combine orange juice, wine, honey, prunes, almonds, raisins and cinnamon in a large saucepan. Bring to a boil, reduce heat to medium and simmer for 5-8 minutes, or until reduced by 1/3.

Add the chicken thigh fillets and continue simmering over low heat, for 10 minutes, or until chicken is just tender. Season to taste with salt and pepper. Serve sprinkled with the parsley and accompanied by couscous or orzo.

Greek Style Chicken Skewers

Serves 4

Ingredients:

1.5 lb chicken breast fillets, cut in bite size pieces

2 tbsp olive oil

1 large lemon, juiced

2 garlic cloves, pressed

1 tsp dried oregano

1 tsp dried rosemary

Directions:

Thread chicken pieces onto skewers. Place in a shallow dish. Combine olive oil and lemon juice, garlic and oregano. Pour over chicken. Turn to coat. Marinate for 40 minutes, if time permits.

Preheat barbecue plate on medium-high heat. Cook skewers for 3 minutes each side or until chicken is just cooked through. Serve with vegetable salad and feta cheese.

Moroccan Chicken with Almond and Spinach Couscous

Serves 4

Ingredients:

4 chicken breast fillets, halved

4 tbsp olive oil

1 tsp saffron

1 tsp nutmeg

1 tsp cinnamon

1 red bell pepper, deseeded, chopped

1 cup baby spinach leaves

1/4 cup slivered almonds

1/4 cup raisins

1 cup chicken broth

1 cup couscous

Directions:

Toss chicken breasts in olive oil and sprinkle with cinnamon, nutmeg and saffron. Heat a frying pan over medium heat. Add the chicken and cook for 4 minutes each side or until golden. Transfer to a baking dish and bake in a preheated to 350 F oven for 10 minutes or until cooked through.

Heat the oil and gently sauté the bell pepper and silvered almonds, stirring, for 2 minutes. Add the raisins and chicken broth and bring to the boil. Remove from heat and add the couscous. Use a fork to combine. Cover and set aside for 2-3 minutes. Use a fork to fluff the grains. Fold through spinach until just wilted. Serve the couscous topped with sliced chicken.

Moroccan Chicken Tagine

Serves 4-5

Ingredients:

1 whole chicken (3-4 lbs), cut into pieces

2 large onions, grated

2 or 3 cloves of garlic, finely chopped or pressed

1 tsp ginger

1 tsp cumin

1 tsp paprika

1 tsp black pepper

1 tsp turmeric

1/2 teaspoon salt

1/2 cup green or black olives, or mixed

1 preserved lemon, quartered and deseeded

5 tbsp olive oil

1 bunch cilantro

1 bunch parsley

Directions:

In a large bowl, mix three tablespoons of olive oil, salt, half the onions, garlic, ginger, cumin, paprika, and turmeric. Mix thoroughly, crush the garlic with your fingers, and add a little water to make a paste.

Roll the chicken pieces into the marinade and leave for 10-15 minutes.

olive oil. Add the chicken and pour excess marinade juices over the top. Add the remaining onions, olives, and chopped preserved lemon. Tie the parsley and cilantro together into a bouquet and place on top of the chicken.

Place the lid on the base, bring to a boil and immediately reduce to a simmer. Cook for 45 minutes, or until the chicken is cooked through and quite tender. Serve with couscous or rice pilaf.

Mediterranean Chicken Couscous

Serves 6

Ingredients:

2 chicken breast halves, cut into strips

2 garlic cloves, finely chopped

1 tbsp freshly ground black pepper

1 cup chicken broth

1 lemon, rind finely grated, juiced

2 cups couscous

1 cup cherry tomatoes, halved

1/2 cup green olives, pitted, halved

1/2 cup fresh parsley leaves, chopped

5-6 spring onions, trimmed, chopped

2 tbs drained capers, chopped

3 tbsp olive oil

Directions:

Marinate the chicken in the oil, garlic and black pepper in a shallow dish. Heat a large saucepan over medium-high heat. Add half the chicken mixture and cook for 2-3 minutes, tossing, until just cooked. Transfer to a plate, cover loosely with foil to keep warm and set aside. Repeat with the remaining chicken mixture.

Increase heat to high and add broth and lemon juice to the pan. Cook, until the liquid comes to the boil. Remove from the heat and add the couscous.

Cover and set aside for 2-3 minutes, or until all the liquid is absorbed. Use a fork to fluff the grains.

Add the chicken, lemon rind, tomatoes, olives, parsley, spring onions and capers. Toss well to combine.

Eggs and Feta Cheese Stuffed Peppers

Serves 4

Ingredients:

8 red bell peppers

6 eggs

4 oz feta cheese

1/2 cup finely cut parsley

2 cups breadcrumbs

1 cup sunflower oil, for frying

Directions:

Grill the peppers or roast them in the oven at 480 F. Peel and deseed the peppers. Mix the crumbled feta cheese with 4 beaten eggs.

Stuff the peppers with the mixture.

Beat the remaining two eggs. Roll each stuffed pepper first in breadcrumbs, then dip in the beaten eggs.

Fry in hot oil turning once. Serve sprinkled with parsley.

Feta Cheese Baked in Foil

Serves 4

Ingredients:

14 oz hard feta cheese

3 oz butter

1 tbsp paprika

1 tsp summer savory

Directions:

Cut the feta cheese into four medium-thick slices and place on sheets of butter-lined foil.

Place cubes of butter on top each feta cheese piece, sprinkle with paprika and savory and wrap. Place in a tray and bake in a moderate oven. Serve wrapped in the foil.

Breaded Cheese

Serves 4

Ingredients:

14 oz feta cheese

2 eggs, beaten

2 tbsp flour

3-4 tbsp bread crumbs

1 cup sunflower oil, for frying

Directions:

Cut the cheese in four equal slices. Dip each piece first in cold water, then roll in the flour, then in the beaten eggs, and finally in the breadcrumbs.

Fry the cheese pieces in preheated oil on both sides. Serve warm.

Bulgarian Baked Beans

Serves 6

Ingredients:

2 cups dried white beans

2 medium onions, chopped

1 red bell pepper, chopped

1 carrot, chopped

1/4 cup sunflower oil

1 tsp paprika

1 tsp black pepper

1 tbsp flour

1/2 cup finely cut parsley

1 tsp salt

Directions:

Wash the beans and soak in water overnight. In the morning discard the water, pour enough cold water to cover the beans, add one of the onions, peeled but left whole. Cook until the beans are soft but not falling apart. If there is too much water left, drain the beans.

Chop the other onion and fry it a frying pan along with the chopped bell pepper and the carrot. Add paprika, flour and the beans. Stir well and pour the mixture in a baking dish along with some parsley, mint, and salt.

Bake in a preheated to 350 F oven for 20-30 minutes. The beans should not be too dry. Serve warm.

Rice Stuffed Bell Peppers

Serves 4

Ingredients:

8 bell peppers, cored and seeded

1 1/2 cups rice, washed and drained

2 onions, chopped

1 tomato, chopped

fresh parsley, chopped

3 tbsp oil

1 tbsp paprika

Directions:

Heat the oil and sauté the onions for 2-3 minutes. Add the paprika, the washed and rinsed rice, the tomato, and season with salt and pepper. Add 1/2 cup of hot water and cook the rice until the water is absorbed.

Stuff each pepper with the mixture using a spoon. Every pepper should be 3/4 full. Arrange the peppers in a deep ovenproof dish and top up with warm water to half fill the dish.

Cover and bake for about 20 minutes at 350 F. Uncover and cook for another 15 minutes until the peppers are well cooked. Serve on their own or with plain yogurt.

Beans Stuffed Bell Peppers

Serves 5

Ingredients:

10 dried red bell peppers

1 cup dried beans

1 onion

3 cloves garlic

2 tbsp flour

1 carrot

1/2 cup finely cut parsley

1/2 crushed walnuts

1 tbsp paprika

salt, to taste

Directions:

Put the dried peppers in warm water and leave them for 1 hour. Cook the beans. Chop the carrot and the onion, sauté them and add them to the cooked beans. Add as well the finely chopped parsley and the walnuts. Stir the mixture to make it homogeneous.

Drain the peppers, then fill them with the mixture and place in a roasting tin, covering the pepper's openings with flour to seal them during the baking. Bake it for about 30 min. at 350 F.

Monastery Stew

Serves 4

Ingredients:

3-4 potatoes, peeled and diced

2-3 tomatoes, diced

1-2 carrots, chopped

1 small onion, chopped

1 celery rib, chopped

2 cups white button mushrooms, chopped

1/2 cup black olives, pitted

1/4 cup rice

1/2 cup white wine

1/3 cup sunflower oil

1/2 cup finely cut parsley

1 tsp black pepper

1 tsp salt

Directions:

Sauté the finely chopped onion, carrots and celery in a little oil. Add olives, mushrooms and black pepper and stir well. Pour over the wine and 1 cup of water, season with salt, cover simmer for 15 minutes.

Add in potatoes, rice, and tomatoes. Transfer everything into an ovenproof casserole, sprinkle with parsley and bake for about 30 minutes at 350 F.

Potato and Leek Stew

Serves 4

Ingredients:

3-4 potatoes, peeled and diced

2-3 leeks, cut into rings

5-6 tbsp olive oil

1/2 cup finely cut parsley

1/2 cup grated yellow cheese (cheddar or Gruyère)

salt, to taste

Directions:

Peel the potatoes, wash them and cut them into small cubes. Slice the leeks. Put the potatoes and the leeks in a pot along with some water and the oil. The water should cover the vegetables.

Season with salt and bring to the boil then simmer until tender. Sprinkle with the finely chopped parsley and the grated yellow cheese.

Spinach with Rice

Serves 4

Ingredients:

3-4 cups fresh spinach, washed, drained and chopped

1/2 cup of rice

1 onion, chopped

1 carrot, chopped

1/4 cup olive oil

2 cups water

Directions:

Heat the oil in a large skillet and cook the onions and the carrot until soft. Add the paprika and the washed and drained rice and mix well. Add two cups of warm water, stirring constantly as the rice absorbs it, and simmer for 10 more minutes.

Wash the spinach well and cut it in strips, then add to the rice and cook until it wilts. Remove from the heat and season to taste. Serve with yogurt.

Stewed Green Beans

Serves 5-6

Ingredients:

2 lb green beans, fresh or frozen

2 onions, chopped

2 garlic cloves, pressed

2 potatoes, peeled and cut in small chunks

2 carrots, sliced

1 cup water

1/2 cup sunflower oil

1 cup finely cut parsley

1/2 cup finely cut dill

1 tsp salt

black pepper, to taste

Directions:

Sauté the onions and the garlic lightly in olive oil. Add the green beans and the remaining ingredients.

Cover and simmer over medium heat for about an hour or until all vegetables are tender. Check after 30 minutes; add more water if necessary. Serve warm, sprinkled with the fresh dill.

Cabbage and Rice Stew

Serves 4

Ingredients:

1 cup long grain white rice

2 cups water

2 tbsp olive oil

1 small onion, chopped

1 garlic clove, pressed

1/4 head cabbage, cored and shredded

2 tomatoes, diced

1 tbsp paprika

1/2 cup finely cut parsley

salt, to taste

black pepper, to taste

Directions:

Heat the olive oil in a large pot. Add the onion and garlic and cook until transparent. Add the paprika, rice and water, stir and bring to boil.

Simmer for 10 minutes. Add the shredded cabbage, the tomatoes, and cook for about 20 minutes, stirring occasionally, until the cabbage cooks down. Season with salt and pepper and serve sprinkled with parsley.

Breakfasts and Desserts

Mediterranean Vegetable Omelette

Serves 5-6

Ingredients:

1 small onion, finely cut

1 green bell pepper, chopped

1 red bell pepper, chopped

4 tomatoes, cubed

2 garlic cloves, pressed

8 eggs

10 oz feta cheese, crumbled

4 tbsp olive oil

1/2 cup finely cut parsley

black pepper, to taste

salt, to taste

Directions:

In a large pan sauté onion over medium heat, till transparent. Reduce heat and add bell peppers and garlic. Continue cooking until soft. Add the tomatoes and continue simmering until the mixture is almost dry.

Add the cheese and all eggs, stir, and cook until well mixed and not too liquid.

Season with black pepper and remove from heat. Sprinkle with parsley.

Feta Cheese Pastry

Serves 6

Ingredients:

14 oz filo pastry

5 eggs

½ cup yogurt

8 oz feta cheese

3.5 oz butter

Directions:

Turn the oven to 350 F. Mix well the eggs, cheese and yogurt in a bowl. Melt the butter in a bowl.

Grease the base of a baking tray, at least 1.5 inch deep, with some of the butter. Take the filo sheets and lay them on a dry surface. Place one sheet of filo pastry in the baking tray. Brush with melted butter using a pastry brush.

Lay another sheet of pastry on top and brush with butter. Sprinkle some of the cheese mixture evenly over the butter-basted pastry. Continue alternating two sheets of butter-basted pastry with the cheese mixture.

Repeat for 6 or 7 layers until all the sheets of pastry have been used up or the pie reaches the top of the baking tray, but make sure you finish with a sheet of pastry on top. If there is any mixture left over brush the top of the Cheese Pastry in the tray, if there is none left - brush some butter.

Place the tray in the oven and bake for 20 minutes until slightly risen and golden. Serve warm.

Spinach-Cheese Pastry

Serves 6-7

Ingredients:

14 oz filo pastry

2 cups washed fresh spinach

2 eggs

1/4 cup sour cream

1/4 cup yogurt

7 oz feta cheese, crumbled

½ cup sunflower oil

1 tsp salt

Directions:

Preheat oven to 350 F. Wash and drain the spinach then chop it and place in a big bowl. Add salt and mix. Leave for about 10 minutes and then drain the excess water. Mix together the eggs, feta cheese and yogurt and add to the spinach. Grease a baking tray, at least 1.5 inch deep.

Take the filo sheets and lay them on a dry surface. Place one sheet of pastry into the baking tray. Brush with oil, using a pastry brush. Place another sheet of pastry on top and brush with oil. Add some filling and spread evenly.

Repeat for 6 or 7 layers until the pie reaches the top but make sure you finish with the pastry on top. Place the Spinach-Cheese Pastry in the oven, uncovered, for about 35 minutes. Take it out of the oven and pour over it 1/4 cup sour cream blended with 1/4 cup of yogurt. Return to the oven and bake for another 15 minutes until golden.

Serve warm or at room temperature.

Pumpkin Pastry

Serves 8

Ingredients:

14 oz filo pastry

1 cups pumpkin, shredded

1 cup walnuts, coarsely chopped

1/2 cup sugar

6 tbsp sunflower oil

1/2 tbsp ground cinnamon

1 tsp vanilla extract

Directions:

Grate the pumpkin and steam it until tender. Cool and add the walnuts, sugar, cinnamon and the vanilla.

Place a few sheets of pastry in the baking dish, sprinkle with oil and spread the filling on top. Repeat this a few times finishing with a sheet of pastry.

Bake for 20 minutes at 350 F. Let the Pumpkin Pie cool down and dust with the powdered sugar.

Strawberry Jam Crêpes

Serves 10

Ingredients:

3 eggs

1/4 cup sugar

2 cups plain flour

2 cups milk

1 large orange, juiced

1/2 tsp vanilla

1/4 cup sunflower oil

1/2 cup strawberry jam

Directions:

Using an electric mixer, lightly beat eggs and 1/4 cup sugar on medium speed until well combined. Add 1/2 cup flour, 1 tablespoon at a time, beating well after each addition. Slowly add remaining 1 1/2 cups flour and milk alternately until batter is smooth. Reduce mixer speed to medium low. Add 1/2 cup orange juice, vanilla and a pinch of salt. Beat until batter is smooth.

Heat a 7 inch base crêpe pan or frying pan over medium heat. Brush pan with a little oil. Pour 2 1/2 tbsp batter into center of pan and swirl to coat base. Cook for 1 to 2 minutes or until base is golden. Turn and cook for 30 seconds. Transfer to a plate. Repeat with remaining batter, greasing pan between crêpes.

Spread one teaspoon of jam over one crêpe. Roll crêpe up tightly. Repeat with remaining crêpes and jam. Layer crêpes on a serving plate. Serve sprinkled with powdered sugar.

French Toast

Serves 4

Ingredients:

8 slices stale bread

4 eggs, beaten

2/3 cup milk

1/2 cup sunflower oil

Directions:

Slice the bread into thin 1/2 inch slices. Dip first in milk, then in the beaten eggs.

Fry in hot oil. Serve hot, sprinkled with sugar, honey, jam, feta cheese or whatever topping you prefer.

Quick Peach Tarts

Serves 4

Ingredients:

1 sheet frozen ready-rolled puff pastry

1/4 cup light cream cheese spread

1 1/2 tablespoons raw sugar

pinch of cinnamon

4 peaches, peeled, halved, stones removed, sliced

Directions:

Preheat oven to 350 F. Line a baking tray with non-stick baking paper. Cut pastry into 4 squares. Place onto prepared tray. Using a spoon, mix cream cheese, one tablespoon of sugar, vanilla and cinnamon. Spread over pastry squares. Arrange peach slices over top.

Bake for 10 minutes or until golden. Sprinkle with remaining sugar and serve.

Baked Apples

Serves 4

Ingredients:

8 medium sized apples

1/3 cup walnuts, crushed

3/4 cup sugar

3 tbsp raisins, soaked

vanilla, cinnamon according to taste

2 oz butter

Directions:

Peel and carefully hollow the apples. Prepare stuffing by beating butter, 3/4 cup of sugar, crushed walnuts, raisins and cinnamon.

Stuff the apples and place in an oiled dish, pour over 1-2 tbsp of water and bake in a moderate oven. Serve warm with a scoop of vanilla ice cream.

Sweet Cheese Balls in Syrup

Serves 6

Ingredients:

3.5 oz feta or cottage cheese

3 eggs

1 cup flour

1 tsp baking soda

1 cup sunflower oil

For the syrup:

3 cups water

3/2 cup sugar

1 tsp vanilla extract

Directions:

Mix the feta cheese and eggs well, before gradually adding the flour, followed by the baking soda. Shape into balls with a spoon and fry in hot oil until golden-brown.

When cooled, pour over syrup made from water, sugar and vanilla.

Caramel Cream

Serves 8

Ingredients:

11/2 cup sugar

4 cups cold milk

8 eggs

2 tsp vanilla powder

Directions:

Melt 1/4 of the sugar in a non-stick pan over low heat. When the sugar has turned into caramel, pour it into 8 cup-sized ovenproof pots covering only the bottoms.

Whisk the eggs with the rest of the sugar and the vanilla, and slowly add the milk. Stir the mixture well and divide between the pots.

Place the 8 pots in a larger, deep baking dish. Pour 3-4 cups of water into the dish. Place the baking dish in a preheated to 280 F oven for about an hour and bake but do not let the water boil, as the boiling will overcook the cream and make holes in it: if necessary, add cold water to the baking dish.

Remove the baking dish from the oven; remove the pots from the dish. Place a shallow serving plate on top, then invert each pot so that the cream unmolds. The caramel will form a topping and sauce.

Bulgarian Rice Pudding

Serves 4

Ingredients:

1 cup short-grain white rice

6 tbsp sugar

1 1/2 cup water

1 1/2 cup whole milk

1 cinnamon stick

1 strip lemon zest

Directions:

Place the rice in a saucepan, cover with water and cook over low heat for about 15 minutes. Add milk, sugar, cinnamon stick and lemon zest and cook over very low heat, stirring frequently until the mixture is creamy. Do not let it boil.

When ready discard the cinnamon stick and lemon zest. Serve warm or at room temperature.

Baklava-Walnut Pie

Serves: 15

Ingredients:

14 oz filo pastry

1 cup ground walnuts

9 oz butter

For the syrup:

2 cups sugar

2 cups water

1 tbsp vanilla powder

2 tbsp lemon zest

Directions:

Grease a baking tray and place 2-3 sheets of pastry. Crush the walnuts and spread some evenly on the pastry. Place two more sheets of the filo pastry on top. Repeat until all the pastry sheets and walnuts have been used up. Always finish with some sheets of pastry on top.

Cut the pie in the tray into small squares. Melt the butter and pour it over the pie. Bake in a preheated oven at 350 F until light brown. When ready set aside to cool.

The syrup: Combine water and sugar in a saucepan. Add vanilla and lemon zest and bring to the boil, then lower the heat and simmer for about 5 minutes until the syrup is nearly thick. Pour hot syrup over the cold baked pie. Leave to stand for at least 1-2 days until completely dry.

FREE BONUS RECIPES: 10 Ridiculously Easy Jam and Jelly Recipes Anyone Can Make

A Different Strawberry Jam

Makes 6-7 11 oz jars

Ingredients:

4 lb fresh small strawberries (stemmed and cleaned)

5 cups sugar

1 cup water

2 tbsp lemon juice or 1 tsp citric acid

Directions:

Mix water and sugar and bring to the boil. Simmer sugar syrup for 5-6 minutes then slowly drop in the cleaned strawberries. Stir and bring to the boil again. Lower heat and simmer, stirring and skimming any foam off the top once or twice.

Drop a small amount of the jam on a plate and wait a minute to see if it has thickened. If it has gelled enough, turn off the heat. If not, keep boiling and test every 5 minutes until ready. Two or three minutes before you remove the jam from the heat, add lemon juice or citric acid and stir well.

Ladle the hot jam in the jars until 1/8-inch from the top. Place the lid on top and flip the jar upside down. Continue until all of the jars are filled and upside down. Allow the jam to cool completely before turning right-side up. Press on the lid to check and see if it has sealed. If one of the jars lids doesn't pop up- the jar is not sealed–store it in a refrigerator.

Raspberry Jam

Makes 4-5 11 oz jars

Ingredients:

4 cups raspberries

4 cups sugar

1 tsp vanilla extract

1/2 tsp citric acid

Directions:

Gently wash and drain the raspberries. Lightly crush them with a potato masher, food mill or a food processor. Do not puree, it is better to have bits of fruit. Sieve half of the raspberry pulp to remove some of the seeds.

Combine sugar and raspberries in a wide, thick-bottomed pot and bring mixture to a full rolling boil, stirring constantly. Skim any scum or foam that rises to the surface. Boil until the jam sets.

Test by putting a small drop on a cold plate – if the jam is set, it will wrinkle when given a small poke with your finger. Add citric acid, vanilla, and stir. Simmer for 2-3 minutes more, then ladle into hot jars. Flip upside down or process 10 minutes in boiling water.

Raspberry-Peach Jam

Makes 4-5 11 oz jars

Ingredients:

2 lb peaches

1 1/2 cup raspberries

4 cups sugar

1 tsp citric acid

Directions:

Wash and slice the peaches. Clean the raspberries and combine them with the peaches is a wide, heavy-bottomed saucepan. Cover with sugar and set aside for a few hours or overnight.

Bring the fruit and sugar to a boil over medium heat, stirring occasionally. Remove any foam that rises to the surface.

Boil until the jam sets. Add citric acid and stir. Simmer for 2-3 minutes more, then ladle into hot jars. Flip upside down or process 10 minutes in boiling water.

Blueberry Jam

Makes 4-5 11 oz jars

Ingredients:

4 cups granulated sugar

3 cups blueberries (frozen and thawed or fresh)

3/4 cup honey

2 tbsp lemon juice

1 tsp lemon zest

Directions:

Gently wash and drain the blueberries. Lightly crush them with a potato masher, food mill or a food processor. Add the honey, lemon juice, and lemon zest, then bring to a boil over medium-high heat.

Boil for 10-15 minutes, stirring from time to time. Boil until the jam sets.

Test by putting a small drop on a cold plate – if the jam is set, it will wrinkle when given a small poke with your finger. Skim off any foam, then ladle the jam into jars. Seal, flip upside down or process for 10 minutes in boiling water.

Triple Berry Jam

Makes 4-5 11 oz jars

Ingredients:

1 cup strawberries

1 cup raspberries

2 cups blueberries

4 cups sugar

1 tsp citric acid

Directions:

Mix berries and add sugar. Set aside for a few hours or overnight. Bring the fruit and sugar to the boil over medium heat, stirring frequently. Remove any foam that rises to the surface. Boil until the jam sets. Add citric acid, salt and stir.

Simmer for 2-3 minutes more, then ladle into hot jars. Flip upside down or process 10 minutes in boiling water.

Red Currant Jelly

Makes 6-7 11 oz jars

Ingredients:

2 lb fresh red currants

1/2 cup water

3 cups sugar

1 tsp citric acid

Directions:

Place the currants into a large pot, and crush with a potato masher or berry crusher. Add in water, and bring to a boil. Simmer for 10 minutes. Strain the fruit through a jelly or cheese cloth and measure out 4 cups of the juice.

Pour the juice into a large saucepan, and stir in the sugar. Bring to full rolling boil, then simmer for 20-30 minutes, removing any foam that may rise to the surface. When the jelly sets, ladle in hot jars, flip upside down or process in boiling water for 10 minutes.

White Cherry Jam

Makes 3-4 11 oz jars

Ingredients:

2 lb cherries

3 cups sugar

2 cups water

1 tsp citric acid

Directions:

Wash and stone cherries. Combine water and sugar and bring to the boil.

Boil for 5-6 minutes then remove from heat and add cherries. Bring to a rolling boil and cook until set. Add citric acid, stir and boil 1-2 minutes more.

Ladle in hot jars, flip upside down or process in boiling water for 10 minutes.

Cherry Jam

Makes 3-4 11 oz jars

Ingredients:

2 lb fresh cherries, pitted, halved

4 cups sugar

1/2 cup lemon juice

Directions:

Place the cherries in a large saucepan. Add sugar and set aside for an hour. Add the lemon juice and place over low heat. Cook, stirring occasionally, for 10 minutes or until sugar dissolves. Increase heat to high and bring to a rolling boil.

Cook for 5-6 minutes or until jam is set. Remove from heat and ladle hot jam into jars, seal and flip upside down.

Oven Baked Ripe Figs Jam

Makes 3-4 11 oz jars

Ingredients:

2 lb ripe figs

2 cups sugar

1 ½ cups water

2 tbsp lemon juice

Directions:

Arrange the figs in a Dutch oven, if they are very big, cut them in halves. Add sugar and water and stir well. Bake at 350 F for about one and a half hours. Do not stir. You can check the readiness by dropping a drop of the syrup in a cup of cold water – if it falls to the bottom without dissolving, the jam is ready. If the drop dissolves before falling, you can bake it a little longer.

Take out of the oven, add lemon juice and ladle in the warm jars. Place the lids on top and flip the jars upside down. Allow the jam to cool completely before turning right-side up.

If you want to process the jams - place them into a large pot, cover the jars with water by at least 2 inches and bring to a boil. Boil for 10 minutes, remove the jars and sit to cool.

Quince Jam

Makes 5-6 11 oz jars

Ingredients:

4 lb quinces

5 cups sugar

2 cups water

1 tsp lemon zest

3 tbsp lemon juice

Directions:

Combine water and sugar in a deep, thick-bottomed saucepan and bring it to the boil. Simmer, stirring until the sugar has completely dissolved. Rinse the quinces, cut in half, and discard the cores. Grate the quinces, using a cheese grater or a blender to make it faster. Quince flesh tends to darken very quickly, so it is good to do this as fast as possible.

Add the grated quinces to the sugar syrup and cook uncovered, stirring occasionally until the jam turns pink and thickens to desired consistency, about 40 minutes. Drop a small amount of the jam on a plate and wait a minute to see if it has thickened. If it has gelled enough, turn off the heat. If not, keep boiling and test every 2-3 minutes until ready. Two or three minutes before you remove the jam from the heat, add lemon juice and lemon zest and stir well.

Ladle in hot, sterilized jars and flip upside down.

About the Author

Vesela lives in Bulgaria with her family of six (including the Jack Russell Terrier). Her passion is going green in everyday life and she loves to prepare homemade cosmetic and beauty products for all her family and friends.

Vesela has been publishing her cookbooks for over a year now. If you want to see other healthy family recipes that she has published, together with some natural beauty books, you can check out her Author Page on Amazon.